For Evan

Enjoy these fantastical T

mayor David McDonald —
2.17.04

email MRM @ MargareTResiMcDonald.com
I will send a more tellsteli versing
a Spoiled little Fellow!

MW00574807

Indonesian Folktales

World Folklore Advisory Board

INDONESIAN FOLKTALES

Retold by Murti Bunanta

Edited by Margaret Read MacDonald

Illustrated by G. M. Sudarta

World Folklore Series

A Member of the Greenwood Publishing Group

Westport, Connecticut • London

Library of Congress Cataloging-in-Publication Data

Indonesian folktales / [compiled by] Murti Bunanta ; edited by Margaret Read MacDonald
; illustrated by G.M. Sudarta.
     p. cm. — (World folklore series)
   Includes bibliographical references and index.
   ISBN 1–56308–909–2 (alk. paper)
   1. Tales—Indonesia. I. Bunanta, Murti, 1946– II. MacDonald, Margaret Read, 1949– III.
Series.
GR320.1473 2003
398.2'09598—dc21   2003053875

British Library Cataloguing in Publication Data is available.

Library of Congress Catalog Card Number: 2003053875
ISBN: 1-56308-909-2

First published in 2003

Libraries Unlimited, Inc., 88 Post Road West, Westport, CT 06881
A Member of the Greenwood Publishing Group, Inc.
www.lu.com

Printed in the United States of America

The paper used in this book complies with the
Permanent Paper Standard issued by the National
Information Standards Organization (Z39.48–1984).

10 9 8 7 6 5 4 3 2 1

Copyright Acknowledgments

Photographs and other illustrations have been used with permission of the following: Julia Aloy; Visi
Anak Bangsa; Agatha Anne Bunanta; T. S. Bunanta; Kartono Ryadi and *Kompas Daily*; Syukri
Ramzan; Untung Syafroni; Endang Roh Suciati; Yusrizal KW; Flora A. Moerdani

With gratitude and happiness,

I dedicate this book to my mother; I always remember the time she shared stories with me

my father, who instilled in me my love of books

my husband, for his love and countless support

Murti Bunanta

World Folklore Series

Indonesian Folktales. Retold by Murti Bunanta. Edited by Margaret Read MacDonald.

Folk Stories of the Hmong: Peoples of Laos, Thailand, and Vietnam. By Norma J. Livo and Dia Cha.

Images of a People: Tlingit Myths and Legends. By Mary Helen Pelton and Jacqueline DiGennaro.

Hyena and the Moon: Stories to Tell from Kenya. By Heather McNeil.

The Corn Woman: Stories and Legends of the Hispanic Southwest. Retold by Angel Vigil.

Thai Tales: Folktales of Thailand. Retold by Supaporn Vathanaprida. Edited by Margaret Read MacDonald.

In Days Gone By: Folklore and Traditions of the Pennsylvania Dutch. By Audrey Burie Kirchner and Margaret R. Tassia.

From the Mango Tree and Other Folktales from Nepal. By Kavita Ram Shrestha and Sarah Lamstein.

Why Ostriches Don't Fly and Other Tales from the African Bush. By I. Murphy Lewis.

The Magic Egg and Other Tales from Ukraine. Retold by Barbara J. Suwyn. Edited by Natalie O. Kononenko.

When Night Falls, Kric! Krac! Haitian Folktales. By Liliane Nerette Louis. Edited by Fred J. Hay.

Jasmine and Coconuts: South Indian Tales. By Cathy Spagnoli and Paramasivam Samanna.

The Enchanted Wood and Other Folktales from Finland. By Norma J. Livo and George O. Livo.

A Tiger by the Tail and Other Stories from the Heart of Korea. Retold by Lindy Soon Curry. Edited by Chan-eung Park.

The Eagle on the Cactus: Traditional Stories from Mexico. Retold by Angel Vigil.

Tales from the Heart of the Balkans. Retold by Bonnie C. Marshall. Edited by Vasa D. Mihailovich.

The Celtic Breeze: Stories of the Otherworld from Scotland, Ireland, and Wales. By Heather McNeil.

Gadi Mirrabooka: Australian Aboriginal Tales from the Dreaming. Retold by Pauline E. McLeod, Francis Firebrace Jones, and June E. Barker. Edited by Helen F. McKay.

Folktales from Greece: A Treasury of Delights. Retold by Soula Mitakidou, Anthony L. Manna, and Melpomeni Kanatsouli.

Selections Available on Audiocassette

Hyena and the Moon: Stories to Tell from Kenya. By Heather McNeil.

The Corn Woman: Stories and Legends of the Hispanic Southwest. Retold by Angel Vigil.

Thai Tales: Folktales of Thailand. Retold by Supaporn Vathanaprida. Edited by Margaret Read MacDonald.

Folk Stories of the Hmong: Peoples of Laos, Thailand, and Vietnam. By Norma J. Livo and Dia Cha.

CONTENTS

Part 1: A General Introduction to Indonesia

Part 2: Food, Games, and Crafts

Part 3: The Tales

PREFACE

This collection contains twenty-nine stories. Thirteen were collected through oral sources, and sixteen were taken from written materials. Ten of the tales with oral sources were collected from my friends, who had heard the stories from their relatives or acquaintances on visits to the sites of the tales' origins. I heard three of the stories from my mother when I was a child.

The sixteen stories retold from written materials were developed by the Department of Education and Culture Project. These were first collected through oral interviews in the languages of the various cultures, then translated into Indonesian, the national language. I believe that twelve of these stories have not been published for the general public before, not even in Indonesian. Certainly most of these tales have not previously been published in children's books in English.

Indonesian folktales have many themes. For the purpose of this book only six are presented: jealous and envious brothers and sisters (stories that teach not to be envious and jealous), stories of independent princesses (an unusual model of strong women characters in folktales), stories of ungrateful children (to teach children to be grateful, obedient, and respect parents from childhood on); stories about rice (because rice is the staple food of most Indonesian people, each ethnic group has its own stories about rice), stories of how things come to be, and legends about places (the legends of places related to the topography of the country).

Indonesia's World Heritage site: The Buddhist Borobudur temple in Central Java, built around A.D. 788. Courtesy of *Kompas Daily*.

ACKNOWLEDGMENTS

I would like to thank the following people, who enthusiastically encouraged me in writing this book. First my thanks go to Margaret, my editor, whom I enjoyed working with. Her cooperation and love for the Indonesian culture are a great contribution to this book.

Thanks to Kartika for her help in entering the manuscript into the computer, which made my work much easier. Thanks to Made Taro for sharing with me a story and game from Bali and providing useful information about it. Thanks to Kartono Ryadi, on the editorial staff of *Kompas Daily,* who has been very helpful in providing many wonderful pictures.

The book is enriched by friends who shared with me the stories they know: G. M. Sudarta, Mr. and Mrs. Aloy, Flora Moerdani, Occa da Lima Meak, Ronidin, Simon Sibon Ola, Frans Hitipeuw, Getruda Trusaka, and Judhy Syarofie. My heartfelt thanks to them.

Thanks also to Yusrizal KW, Suyadi, and Denny Djoenaid for their information on the culture and to Heang Winoto for the jackfruit seed recipe.

Grateful appreciation also to the people and institutions who have provided me with the pictures I needed for this book. And thanks to G. M. Sudarta for the illustrations based on Indonesian folk motifs.

MAP OF INDONESIA

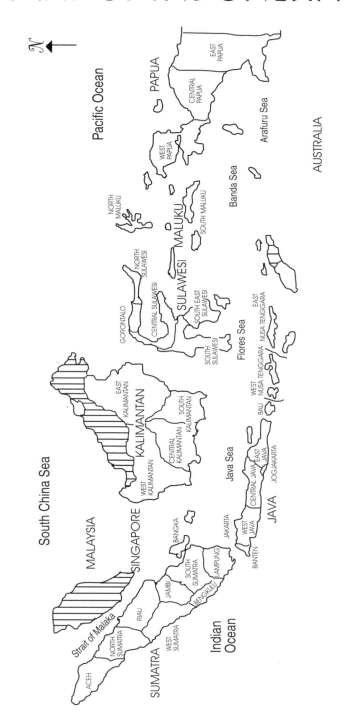

PART 1

A GENERAL INTRODUCTION
TO INDONESIA

THE LAND

*I*ndonesia is an archipelago consisting of more than 17,500 islands that stretch out along the equator for over 5,000 kilometers (3,125 miles). Of this number, 6,044 islands have been named. Only half of the islands are inhabited. The five main islands are Sumatera, Java, Kalimantan, Sulawesi, and Papua (formerly Irian Jaya). Indonesia is subdivided into thirty-two provinces. This number will increase as more regions gain their autonomy from the central government. In 2001 six new provinces were established.

The total area encompassed by Indonesia is 9.8 million square kilometers (3.8 million square miles), but 81 percent of that is sea. From west to east Indonesia is longer than the distance between the east and west coasts of the United States.

THE PEOPLE

*I*ndonesia's population of 220 million is divided among 300 ethnic groups. Jakarta is the capital. Its modernization and economic development have attracted hundreds of thousands of people from all over the country to seek a better fortune. This has caused the city's population to grow to approximately 15 million inhabitants.

The biggest ethnic group is the Javanese, who live in East and Central Java and form 47 percent of the population. During the Dutch colonial occupation many Javanese were moved to Sumatera, Sulawesi, and Kalimantan islands because of a shortage of labor on those islands. This policy of relocating people to other islands is being continued by the Indonesian government. As a result, ethnic groups often mingle with local communities.

This multi-ethnic, multicultural, and multireligious society is united by the country's philosophy, "Bhinneka Tunggal Ika," which means "Unity in Diversity." The diversity is enriched by Arabs, Indians, and Chinese, who have been living in Indonesia for many generations and whose cultures have blended with the local cultures.

LANGUAGE

*T*he national language is Bahasa Indonesia (Language of Indonesia). This has roots in the Malay language, which is spoken by the Riau people in Sumatera. There are also more than 800 other languages and dialects spoken in Indonesia. For example, on Kalimantan the Dayak people, who have the largest population on the island, can be grouped into seven large ethnic groups. These seven ethnic groups consist of 409 subgroups. Each subgroup has its own dialect. Sometimes even a language that is spoken only by a very small number of people has more than one dialect.

Some languages have several "levels." There is language that is used among close friends or to address someone who is either younger or lower in social status. Another form of language is used when speaking to older people or to those of a higher status. There is also a combination of those two forms. Sometimes there is even a palace language, spoken only around royalty.

Major languages are Javanese, Sundanese, Madurese, Balinese, Malay, Amboinese, and Minahasa, spoken by groups of the same names. Several languages are endangered, as they are spoken only by a small number of people and have not yet been written down. Other languages are used only in ceremonies and are not understood by the young generation anymore. The national language, Bahasa Indonesia, is widely used as the medium of communication. This helps unite the various ethnic groups.

A BRIEF HISTORY

Prehistoric

Archeological findings show that Indonesia has a long human history. Fossil remains of Java Man (*Homo erectus*), who lived in Java 1.7 million years ago, have been located in Central Java. Solo Man *(Homo soloenis)* is believed to be the evolutionary descendent of *Homo erectus*. Solo Man inhabited Central Java 250,000 years ago.

Around 5,000 B.C. Austronesian people began to move into Indonesia from what is now the Philippines. The reconstruction of the early stages of Austronesian languages suggests that the Austronesians are the direct ancestors of the Indonesian people.

The period from 500 B.C. to A.D. 500 is called the Dong Son Bronze Age because of the use of ceremonial bronze and iron objects that were made in the tradition called Dong Son, which spread from northern Vietnam.

Hindu

The Classic period, A.D. 400–1500, was marked by the influence of Indian civilization. In A.D. 400 two Hindu kingdoms emerged, Tarumanegara in West Java and Kutai in East Kalimantan. Stone inscriptions have been found in this area written in the South Indian *pallawa* script.

Hindu and Buddhist

In Central Java the ancient Hindu and Buddhist kingdoms ruled from the eighth to the tenth centuries. The Sanjayas were Sivaistic Hindus and the Sailendras were Mahayana Buddhists. Many great monuments were built during this period. Hindu architecture includes the great Siva temple, Prambanan, and the temples of the Dieng Plateau. Buddhist architecture can be seen in the large temple, Borobudur, Sewu (one thousand temple), and Mendut . These are located in Central Java.

Sriwijaya

In the Middle Classic period the most prominent Buddhist kingdom was Sriwijaya in Sumatera, ruled by the Sailendra family, who fled to that place after the Sanjaya dynasty seized control of Central Java around A.D. 832–856.

The golden age of Sriwijaya continued until the eleventh century. In East Java, Kadiri and Singasari were the most prominent kingdoms. The kings of Kadiri were Hindus, whereas the kings of Singasari combined Hinduism and Buddhism.

Majapahit

The Late Classic period, from the fourteenth to the sixteenth centuries, was marked by the rise of Majapahit, which succeeded Singasari in the late thirteenth century. This Indonesian empire was the largest ever to form in Southeast Asia. Majapahit society achieved significant political, literary, commercial, diplomatic, and artistic advancements. The fourteenth century was considered the "golden age" of Majapahit.

Islam

In the fifteenth century the Majapahit and Kadiri were conquered by the Islamic state of Demak on Java's north coast, and the entire Hindu-Javanese aristocracy fled to Bali. Islam gradually spread. In the early sixteenth century the coastal kingdoms of Java were mostly converted to Islam.

Dutch and Japanese Occupations

In 1596 the first Dutch ships dropped anchor in Banten (West Java). The Dutch colonial occupation lasted 350 years. In 1942 the Japanese invaded, leaving in 1945 at the end of World War II.

The Indonesian leaders Sukarno and Mohamad Hatta declared Indonesia's independence as a republic in 1945. In 1949 the Dutch finally acknowledged Indonesia's independence.

The new republic comprised twenty-five provinces, and in 1962 Irian Jaya (now named Papua) was integrated into Indonesia as the twenty-sixth province. In 1976 Indonesia annexed East Timor, but in 1999 East Timor voted for independence. In 2001 six regions received autonomy from the central government, so that Indonesia is now divided into thirty-two provinces.

RELIGION AND CUSTOMS

*T*here are four religions in Indonesia: Islam, Christianity, Buddhism, and Hinduism. Nearly 90 percent of Indonesians are followers of the Islamic religion. Indonesia now has the world's largest Muslim population. Indonesia is not, however, an Islamic state. Religious tolerance and freedom of religion are guaranteed by the constitution and ensured by the *Pancasila* creed, so that Indonesians are free to follow their own faith.

Hinduism in Indonesia differs from Indian Hinduism because of its local characteristics, combining Buddhism, Hinduism, and animistic beliefs. The Balinese religion is known as Hindu Dharma or Agama Hindu. Hinduism is also practiced on the island of Lombok. Hindu Kaharingan is practiced by the Dayak Malaris people in Kalimantan, and Hindu Tenggerese is practiced by the Tengger people, who live in the mountain range of Tengger in East Java.

Most Buddhists in Indonesia are Chinese, whose religion also includes Taoism and Confucianism. A great number of Christians can be found among the Batak people in North Sumatera, the Amboinese in Maluku, the Florinese in Flores, the Minahasan in North Sulawesi, the Dayak in Kalimantan, and the Papuans in Papua. Animism is sometimes still practiced in remote areas.

Each ethnic group has its own *adat,* or local custom, which has been passed from generation to generation and influences the practice of religion. Many rituals are still performed and are an integral part of life. These might mark rites of passage, such as pregnancy, birth, marriage, death, anniversary, or circumcision, or they could mark such events as initiating a new building, celebrating the harvest, or honoring one's ancestors.

PERFORMING ARTS
AND MUSIC

*E*ach Indonesian ethnic group has its own dance, theater, and storytelling traditions. These performances are an integral part of cultural life. Java has the oldest known dance and theater traditions in Indonesia. Stone inscriptions and bas-relief of temples from the eighth and ninth centuries depict dancing and musical entertainment. In the past, kingdoms maintained palace dance and theatrical troupes. These are now found only in Central Java. There were also court dances, traditionally performed only by princesses or daughters of the ruling family.

The shadow puppet play called *wayang kulit*, using flat leather puppets, is popular in Java. The body of the leather puppet is perforated and painted, then provided with movable arms. The play usually performs *Ramayana* and *Mahabharata* stories. In West Java the puppet theater is called *Wayang Golek* and uses doll puppets made from wood. Another kind of doll puppet theater, *Wayang Klitik,* is performed in Central and East Java. The stories presented in *Wayang Klitik* theater are about local kingdoms. Puppet theaters are also found in Bali. In Lombok the puppet theater is known as *Wayang Sasak;* flat leather puppets are used to perform Islamic stories. There are several kinds of folk theater played by actors on a stage, such as *Wayang Topeng* (mask drama), *Wayang Orang* (dance drama), and *Ketoprak* (also dance drama, but the performances can be drawn from any stories). *Barong*, elaborate costumed dances now popular with tourists, are performed in Bali.

Gamelan music from Indonesia is recognized as one of the world's most sophisticated musical arts. Most of the instruments used are percussive, and the music accompanies dance and theater performances.

ARTS AND CRAFTS

*I*ndonesia is known for its handicrafts, which vary from traditional arts and crafts to modern arts. The choices are remarkable: puppets, masks, woodcarvings, stone and metal statues, gold and silver work, basketry, pottery, textiles, painting, and other contemporary arts.

Indonesian arts and crafts are not primarily made to be souvenirs. For Indonesians they serve as part of social and cultural identity. The island of Lombok is well known for its earthenware pottery. The Javanese are known for their *batik*, art on fabric. The Asmat of Irian Jaya have the most impressive primitive art on woodcarvings.

Arts and crafts are also used as a manifestation of spiritual beliefs. Wood statues are placed in the homes of newly married couples in the hope for happiness. Ceremonial masks are used to protect against evil spirits. Functional objects, such as basketry used for fishing traps, hats, and containers, can also be art objects, as can pottery bowls and water pitchers. Wood carvings are used for decoration on fine furniture. Traditional jewelry made of gold and silver is customary as a bride gift.

TEXTILES

*E*ach ethnic group has its own unique textiles, which have value and meaning for the community and are not simply clothing. The creation and use of textiles are connected to cultural background and beliefs. Some textile items are considered sacred cloths and used only for ceremonies and ritual purposes.

Batik textiles are created by marking the fabric with wax, then dipping it into dye. When the wax is removed, the area covered by wax is un-dyed, creating a pattern in the fabric. *Batik tulis* (written *batik*) is made individually by drawing with a special tool. *Batik cap* (printed *batik*) is made in the factory using blocks to print the design. In the past certain motifs were only worn and designed for the royal family.

Ikat or woven cloth can be found in North Sumatera and Sumba Island. Palembang, in South Sumatera province, is well known for its *Songket*, material that has gold or silver threads. The Dayak people are known for their *Ulap Doyo*, material made from leaf fibers of the Doyo plant, and the Batak people are known for their *Ulos,* made from pineapple fibers.

STORYTELLING

*T*raditional storytelling takes place everywhere throughout the archipelago. Each ethnic group has its own art of storytelling. These performances will last hours, beginning in the evening and continuing until dawn. In some cases a performance may continue over several nights.

In rural areas performances are presented for entire communities, including children. In the cities only rarely do children watch traditional storytelling performances. The presentation can be recited or sung by a storyteller, accompanied by music and sometimes also dance. Storytelling performance types include *Kaba,* by the Minangkabau in West Sumatera; *hoho,* by the Ono Niha in Nias Island; *didong,* by the Gayo people in Aceh in North Sumatera; and *kentrung,* by the Javanese in East Java.

Some storytelling performances use puppet theater, such as Javanese *Wayang Kulit* (shadow puppet), Sundanese *Wayang Golek* (wooden puppet), and *Wayang Klitik* (in Central Java and East Java). *Wayang Kulit* puppets are made from perforated leather, *Wayang Golek* are wooden, doll-like puppets, and *Wayang Klitik* use wood for the bodies and leather for the arms.

The stories could include tales from the *Mahabarata* and *Ramayana,* stories about local kingdoms, the origin of gods, humans, and the universe, or folktales and religious stories.

These tales are intended to teach religion; to disseminate local customs, traditions, and morals; and to introduce their folk heroes and history to the community and the younger generation. In many cases storytelling is used in ceremonies such as those for pregnancy, circumcision, and marriage. And of course another function is to entertain.

Storytelling still takes place in homes today. In the cities it takes the form of bedtime stories or reading aloud. Not all families have the habit of it, regardless of their status, and no set stories are told. In the rural areas, in some cases, during the full moon or after sunset prayers is when older family members (mother, father, or grandparents) tell stories to the children in the neighborhood. At bedtime stories are told to their own children. The stories that are most widely known by children in rural areas are about local heroes and legends about places in the neighborhood. Other stories used are about the origins of ancestors, fables, and those that relate to their religion.

PART 2

FOOD, GAMES, AND CRAFTS

FOOD

$\mathcal{T}$he variety of Indonesian food is absolutely incredible. Each culture, each region, each town, and each village has a specialty. Some of these are enjoyed nationwide; others have all but disappeared because they don't please the modern taste. Some Indonesian dishes known internationally are *gado-gado* (salad), *satay* (chicken barbeque), and *nasi goreng* (fried rice).

There are also foods made only for a special purpose or occasion, such as a ceremonial meal. In the past some foods were only served to a particular rank of people, such as nobles and the royal family. Some of these now have become popular foods for everyone.

One unique aspect of Indonesian food is the naming of the dishes. *Ketoprak* is a kind of salad; the name refers to a drama depicting historical events. *Abug macan ubi kayu*, made from cassava, means "tiger cake." *Kue biji nangka*, a cake made from potatoes, is called "jackfruit seed cake." *Granat muncrat* is a small, round cake filled with red sugar that will spurt out in the mouth when it is eaten. The name means "spurt grenade."

The following recipes—a drink, (*Wedang Tomat*), a snack (*Kue Biji Nangka*), and a pudding (*Agar Agar Santan*)—demonstrate the richness of Indonesian folk food.

Wedang Tomat

This is a recipe for a delicious tomato drink from Rembang, a small town in Central Java.

Ingredients:

3 ripe tomatoes

2 cups boiling water

2 tablespoons sugar

Instructions:

1. Cut the tomatoes into small pieces and put them in a glass. Add the sugar.
2. Pour in the boiled water and stir.
3. Serve warm.

Kue Biji Nangka

This is a jackfruit seed cake from South Sulawesi.

Ingredients:

    4 large potatoes

    12 tablespoons ground almond

    1 ½ cups sugar

    ½ teaspoon vanilla

    1 egg white

    4 eggs, separated

    1 ⅙ cups (300 cc) water

Instructions:

1. Cook the potatoes, peel them, then mash them.
2. Add the almond and ⅖ cup (100 grams) of the sugar to the mashed potato and heat on low. Stir until it is dry and can be shaped with the hands. It should not be sticky.

3. Form the batter into cylindrical pieces shaped like a jackfruit seed.

4. In a saucepan, combine the remaining sugar with the vanilla and egg whites until completely mixed. Add the water and bring to a boil.

5. Turn down the heat but keep the mixture warm.

6. In a large bowl, beat the egg yolks.

7. Dip the jackfruit shapes into the egg yolk until completely covered.

8. Put the jackfruit shapes into the warm mixture of sugar, vanilla, and egg whites. Cook until the yolk hardens.

9. Remove the jackfruit seed cakes one by one and drain.

Agar Agar Santan

This is a treat from Central Java.

Ingredients:

4 tablespoons unflavored gelatin

1 ½ cups coconut milk

3 ½ cups water

1 ½ cups sugar

1 teaspoon salt

Food coloring or syrup

Instructions:

1. Mix all ingredients and bring to a boil over medium heat, stirring often.

2. Pour into a mold.

3. Let cool, then refrigerate.

4. Cut into small pieces to serve

Note: This pudding will consist of two layers. The top should be opaque and the bottom should be clear.

GAMES

*T*he richness of Indonesian folklore can be seen in the variety of traditional children's games that are played, particularly in the rural areas. These are part of the children's daily activities, in addition to schooling, religious activities, and helping their parents.

These games are closely related to the natural surroundings in which the children live. Stones, sticks, seeds, leaves, fruits, soil, sand, and things that are easily found at home such as rubber bands, paper, and small pieces of broken tile are used. Traditional Indonesian games may look simple, but they require great physical skill and dexterity.

Games from various parts of Indonesia are presented here. Some, like hide and seek, are similar in every region. This game has many variations and has a different name in each region. In Bali it is popular as *Alih-Alihan*; in Ambarawa, a small town in Central Java, it is called *Tong Mok*; in West Java people call it *Ucing Sumput*; in West Kalimantan it is known as *Sam Khong*; in Lampung it is called *Petak Umpet*; and in East Java it is *Obak Dele*. Hopscotch is also a very common game in every region.

Alih-Alihan

This game comes from Southern Bali. The same game in Northern Bali is called *Kring-Kringan*. The players begin with a counting out ritual. If only two players are involved in the game, the players face each other and say "sut." On the word "sut," each player holds up a thumb, an index finger, or a little finger. The thumb is the "elephant." The index finger is a "human." The little finger is an "ant." The elephant conquers the human, and the human conquers the ant. But the ant conquers the elephant, because ants can crawl into the ears of elephants and annoy them.

If more than two players are involved, the players say "Hom Pim PA." They form a circle, and on the word "pa" each puts forward the top or bottom of the hand. If one player has chosen a different side from all the other players, that player is out. The process continues until only two players are left. Then those two do the "sut" to decide who is "it."

Alih-Alihan **Hide and Seek**

"It" covers his or her face and counts up to an agreed upon number while the others hide. When "it" finds a hiding player, "it" calls that player's name and runs back to the "fortress" post. "It" must reach the "fortress" before the hiding player. If other players can sneak in and reach the "fortress," this means that the "it" player remains the same. A round continues until all players are found. The first player caught becomes "it" for the next round.

Sengge

This game is from Lamalera village in East Nusa Tenggara. It is for two or more players. The game is played barefoot on the beach or in a yard. Mark a line for the start and finish. Each player puts a small stone on top of one foot. At a signal, all players try to hop to the finish line without dropping the stone.

Bala-Bala Tumban

This game comes from La'bo village in South Sulawesi Province and is for three or more players. Girls especially love this game. The players stand in a circle with their backs toward each other. Each hooks one leg on another player's leg. They then jump with the other leg and move in a circle. While jumping the players will clap and sing the *"bala-bala tumban"* chant (below). It is great fun to jump around in a circle while trying to hold the hook and not drop the legs.

Chant:

> *Bala-bala tumban, tumban terasi.*
>
> *Pira tarasimi, sangapulo ringgi.*
>
> *Ben oa misa, kutu tukani.*
>
> *Sereku meong . . . meong . . . meong.*

Instructions:

1. The first player lifts up one leg and bends it.
2. The second player puts a leg on the first player's leg.
3. The third player locks the hook by putting one leg in under the first player's leg and sticking it out above the second player's leg.

Kirek, Kirek Ganjing, a Lampung version of Bala-Bala Tumban, from La'bo village in South Sulawesi Province. It is played primarily by girls. Photograph by Suandi Bunanta.

Hooking the legs in *Bala-Bala Tumban* or *Kirek, Kirek Ganjing*. Photograph by Suandi Bunanta.

Part 2: Food, Games, and Crafts

CRAFTS

*I*ndonesian crafts are not only those created by masters, such as silver work, wood carving, sculpture, and other sophisticated crafts, but also those found in daily life. The wrappers used for foods are an unusual Indonesian craft that has many variations. Banana, coconut, lontar, and other leaves are used. Food wrapping varies from simple to a very complicated container that requires skill and perseverance to create.

During the Muslim New Year the main treat is *ketupat,* which is served with many other dishes. Ketupat is made of steamed rice wrapped in coconut leaves. There are at least thirty different types. This tradition has been passed from generation to generation.

Ketupat, decorated with striped ribbons and wrappers made from coconut leaves.
Photograph by Suandi Bunanta.

A children's craft using a pomelo (or a thick-skinned grapefruit) skin to make a boat and a vehicle is described below. A raft made from straws is also described.

Pomelo Skin Boat

Instructions:

1. Slice a round piece off the top of the pomelo.
2. Cut the fruit vertically into six or seven pieces of about the same size.
3. Remove the inside of the fruit.
4. Use one piece of pomelo rind for the body of the boat.
5. To make a boat, embed one wooden or plastic stick upright as a mast.
6. Cut paper in the shape of a triangle to use as the sail and glue it onto the stick.

Now your boat is ready to sail in a pond or stream.

Pomelo Skin Vehicle

Instructions:

1. Use one piece of pomelo skin for the body of the vehicle.
2. Take another piece of skin and cut the small point off the end. Discard the small piece.
3. Divide the rest of that piece of skin into two pieces. Cut these into circles to make wheels.
4. Push a stick through the body piece horizontally so that it sticks out on both sides. Attach the wheels.
5. Pierce one end of the body and attach a small cord or string.

Your vehicle is now ready to go.

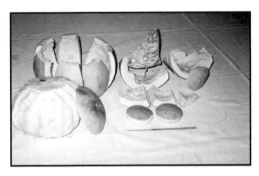

It is simple to create a boat or a vehicle from a pomelo skin. Photograph by Suandi Bunanta.

Pomelo skin boat (left) and vehicle (right). Photograph by Suandi Bunanta.

Part 2: Food, Games, and Crafts

Raft from Straws

Instructions:

1. Lay out twenty straws evenly next to each other on a flat surface.

2. Place one straw across each end of the row of straws and glue both in place.

3. To make a small seat to ride on the raft, cut ten straws in half and lay them out next to each other.

4. Place half of a straw across each end of the row of half straws and glue both in place.

5. Place the seat on top of the raft, with the two cross straws on the bottom.

Your raft is ready to sail in the bathtub.

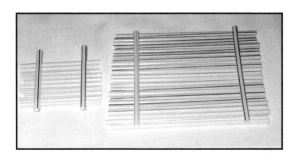

Raft (right) and seat (left).
Photograph by Suandi Bunanta.

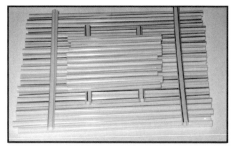

Finished straw raft, ready to sail.
Photograph by Suandi Bunanta.

PART 3

THE TALES

Jealous and Envious Brothers and Sisters

One of the main morals taught in Indonesian folktales is not to be envious and jealous of your brothers and sisters. These four folktales deal with this problem in a somewhat humorous manner.

TATTADU

A folktale from South Sulawesi, collected in the regional language, Duri Massenrengpulu

A long time ago, there lived seven sisters. The youngest had not been married yet. Every day her sisters would mock her. "Look at you! No man is willing to marry you. No one will ever marry you!"

One day Youngest Sister went to a well to draw water. Around the well grew a grove of taro trees. In those taro trees, thousands of *tattadu* (caterpillars) were nestling among the leaves. The girl was very unhappy because of the teasing of her sisters. She spoke out loud and said, "Every day I am mocked by my sisters. If only some one would ask to marry me, I would accept the proposal . . . , even if it were nothing more than a *tattadu*!"

Now one of the *tattadu* hiding among the taro tree leaves heard what the girl had said. When she went home that *tattadu* followed her.

After a while the girl stopped. The *tattadu* quickly climbed up onto her leg. Now it could ride home with her more easily. But the girl noticed the caterpillar and brushed it off.

The next time she paused for a moment, up climbed the *tattadu* again. "What are you doing, *tattadu*? Stay off of my leg!"

How surprised she was when the caterpillar spoke. "You just said you would marry anyone, even if it was a *tattadu*. I have come to marry you."

The girl realized she had made a mistake to speak in that way. But she didn't know how to get rid of the *tattadu*.

When the girl arrived back home with a caterpillar, her sisters didn't know what to think. "Why did you bring home that *tattadu?*"

"It is my destiny. I am married now. To this *tattadu*. You can stop teasing me, because I am married." The girl had reconciled herself to this fate.

From that time, Tattadu lived at Youngest Sister's house. One day he spoke to his wife, "Dear wife, I will be going far away into the woods to start a farm. While I am gone, stay at home. I promise to return after my farm has yielded its crops.

Early in the morning, Tattadu went into the dense forest. It took him quite some time to reach the forest, crawling slowly as he did. Once there he began to gnaw on the trees. One by one he gnawed until each tree fell. Eventually he had cleared enough land to plant a farm. Then he planted crops and waited for them to grow.

Very quickly, as if by magic, three pumpkin vines sprang up and began to creep over the entire farm, covering everything. When they began to bear, Tattadu picked one of the pumpkins. When he cut it open . . . it was full of gold and jewelry!

"Perhaps a god has given this wonderful crop to me. I must go home and carry the pumpkins to my wife," muttered Tattadu.

How delighted Youngest Sister was when her husband came home bringing such treasure. Now her sisters did not dare to laugh at her and her strange husband.

But Tattadu didn't remain at home with her for long. "Dear wife, I must travel again. I am going to a far land. Perhaps I can change my appearance. You must have great patience and wait for my return as before."

Tattadu traveled to a faraway land. There people were able to mold all sorts of animals and humans. They could shape dogs, pigs, humans . . . whatever was wanted.

When Tattadu arrived, the god asked him, "Why do you come here, Tattadu?"

"Please forgive me," replied Tattadu. "I come here in order to change my looks. The appearance I now have causes my wife to be mocked by her sisters. They laugh that my wife is married to a caterpillar. I beg you to change my form into that of a human."

After listening to Tattadu, the god spoke, "Now, choose for yourself the molding you like. If you are lucky, you will change into a human as you wish. But if you have no luck, you will change into the form of the mold you have entered."

Tattadu thanked the god and, selecting the mold he thought looked most promising, he entered. Indeed, he had chosen wisely. He changed into a human. But unfortunately this human form had no head!

"Well, Tattadu," said the god. "Climb this tree." But as he was climbing, people began to mock and laugh. "Look at that bizarre man without a head!"

So the god told him to enter the mold again.

This time he came out with a handsome head *and* the body of a strong man with regal bearing.

"Go climb the tree again," said the god.

This time as he was climbing the tree, people began to call, "Why is that king climbing a tree? Why doesn't he send his servant to fetch what he wants?"

The god listened to this and told Tattadu, "Tattadu, go home. You are ready to return to your wife. Here is some rice wine for your journey. If you use it wisely it will never become empty."

So Tattadu set off for his home village. On the way he met a village chief. "What are you carrying there, Tattadu?" The chief had seen the bottle of rice wine. "Could you give me a little?"

"This is a special rice wine," replied Tattadu "I can give you some. But I will set a condition. If you finish all of the wine, I will become your servant. But if you fail to finish it, you and your entire village will become *my* servants."

The chief liked this wager. He grabbed the bottle of wine and began to drink. Of course, no matter how long and deeply he drank, he could not finish the wine. Eventually the chief had to admit defeat and turn over his entire village to Tattadu.

So Tattadu started on for his home village, bringing an entourage of servants with him. In each of the three villages he passed en route, he met up with greedy chiefs who desired his rice wine. And at each village he made the same wager and ended up with a village of servants.

In the meantime, back at home, Youngest Sister had been constantly praying for her husband's return. She sang of his return in hopeful words:

"My caterpillar is coming,

Swaying like a worm,

Walking in procession with his servants,

Followed by his cattle."

Her sisters mocked her singing and her prayers. "Don't dream. Your husband is long dead. He won't come back."

When Tattadu arrived at the village with his entourage of servants, the villagers thronged to see. They thought this was a wealthy king who had come to their village.

As word of the rich king's arrival reached Tattadu's home, her sisters ordered her to go to her room. "You will only embarrass us when the king sees you," they said. So Youngest Sister remained at home, and her sisters hurried to meet the king. Approaching him, they offered betel leaves and areca nuts on a silver plate. But the king would not touch their gifts. The sisters hurried home and put the betel onto a gold plate. Then they returned again. Still the king declined their gifts.

Suddenly the crowd parted. There was Youngest Sister. She was carrying an old and worn plate. On it was her offering of betel. The king's face gleamed with happiness as he bent forward and accepted her gift.

When the sisters realized that this was Tattadu, Youngest Sister's caterpillar husband, they were amazed. "How did you become such a handsome king?"

"I traveled to a faraway land where the god molds creatures. With the god's permission I was remolded into the human you now see before you."

The sisters were so envious that they ordered their own husbands to go at once to that faraway land and get themselves remolded into a handsomer form.

When the husbands arrived, the god asked, "What is your intention in coming here?"

"We come to be remolded and become as handsome as Tattadu," said the husbands. "Our wives demand it."

"All right, if that is what you want," replied the god. "Choose a mold to enter. But be careful. If you are lucky, you will emerge handsomer. But if you are not lucky, you might end up changed into an animal."

The husbands each chose a mold and entered. But disaster! They each emerged, not as a handsome man, but as an abject animal!

Miserable and ashamed, they returned home. When their wives saw these ugly animals arriving, they did not recognize them. "Get out! What are you dirty animals doing trying to get into the house? You will foul the house!"

"But we are your husbands. It is because of your jealousy that we have become like this. This must be the punishment for those who are too greedy and selfish," replied the six husbands.

Now the wives regretted their actions. But nothing could be done. It had happened. It was impossible for their husbands to become human again. Only once could they be allowed to remold their appearance.

So the sisters received the punishment they deserved. They lived in grief and disgrace married to men in the form of animals.

Youngest Sister lived happily from then on with her noble and rich husband. Yet her character had not changed. She remained kind and humble. And her neighbors loved and respected her.

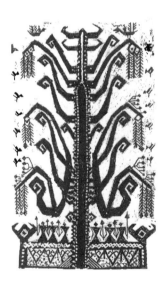

Part 3: The Tales

BUJANG PERMAI

A folktale from Pasar Baru Regency in West Sumatera

In a village there once lived a husband and wife with their three sons. The oldest son's name was Dahar, the middle was Dahir, and the youngest was Bujang Permai.

One day the parents went to the market to sell their crops. But just after they had crossed over the bridge, it was suddenly smashed by a flood. Days passed and they could not return home since there was no other way to cross the river. After waiting for a long time for their return, the three sons decided that their parents must have died. They sorrowed over the loss of their parents.

One night the two older sons decided to go seek their fortune in other lands. They didn't have the heart to leave their little brother, Bujang Permai, alone in the village, so they agreed to take him along with them. The next day very early in the morning, the three brothers left their home to look for a better future.

After a long walk, the brothers arrived at the edge of a village. They found a small, empty hut and rested there. While resting, each brother began to talk of his deepest wishes.

Dahar, the eldest, said, "I will look for a rich landlord with a huge farm. There I will plant vegetables, cassava, black pepper, and beans near my hut. Then I will not have to worry about my daily life as I will have everything I need ready at hand."

Dahir, the second son, spoke next, "As for me, I will find a landlord who has a lot of water buffaloes. I will herd them the whole day and take good care of them. Every morning I will milk them and every day I will eat the *dadih** (buffalo yogurt) and drink the milk."

Now that they had revealed their own wishes, the two brothers urged Bujang Permai to tell his wish. At first he refused. Eventually he said, "I want to become a king. I will look for a beautiful wife. Everyone will honor me."

Listening to the proud wishes of Bujang Permai, his two brothers were angered. They thought Bujang Permai was mocking them, while they had told him their true wishes. Angrily they tied Bujang Permai to a post in the hut and left him there.

---

* *Dadih* is a fermented water buffalo milk. People eat it like yogurt or served with some side dishes. This fermented milk is made in the joints of bamboo.

"Be a king then," said Dahar. "Find your beautiful wife *here.*"

The two brothers continued their journey, leaving Bujang Permai alone tied up in the little hut. After a time the two brothers arrived in a village. There they met a well off farmer. They were able to obtain work with the rich family, just as they had hoped. Dahar was hired as a farmer and Dahir as a breeder of water buffaloes.

In the night they were already in their hut resting when they suddenly remembered their youngest brother. They had left him tied up and alone. They realized he might be in danger. A fierce animal might have attacked him. And who would feed him? He had been tied up all day long. They could not sleep that night.

Very early in the morning, they asked their landlord permission to go back and find their brother. They ran helter-skelter toward the hut where they had left Bujang Permai. But when they arrived, their youngest brother was not there. They looked for him everywhere, but in vain. Finally they had to give up. Sad and regretful, they returned to their landlord.

But what had happened to Bujang Permai? After his brothers left, Bujang Permai had tried very hard to loosen the knots with which he was tied. As they were too tight, he failed to loosen them and fell into an exhausted sleep.

In his exhaustion, he began to dream. In his dream, he saw an old man come to him. The old man had a long beard reaching to the ground. He was dressed all in white. He spoke, "Bujang Permai, you don't need to look for your brothers and follow them. Tomorrow a bird will come to fetch you. Continue your journey and follow the direction it flies. I will leave seven palm leaf ribs beside you. They have magical power. These palm leaf ribs can make the dead come to life again." After uttering this, the old man disappeared from the dream.

When Bujang Permai woke up the following day, he discovered that he was already untied. Beside him he found seven palm leaf ribs, just as the old man had said. In a little while he heard a bird's song.

Now Bujang Permai did as the old man had told him. He followed the bird wherever it flew. When the bird flew through the air, Bujang Permai followed along. In the night the bird would perch on a branch and Bujang Permai would sleep under the tree.

Traveling this way, Bujang Permai wandered for three months through the forest. One day he came across a dead macaque on the path. Bujang Permai repeated the magic spells he had learned from the old man in the dream. Then he whisked the macaque with the palm leaf ribs. The macaque came to life again!

As a token of his gratitude the macaque gave Bujang Permai a gift of incense. "If ever you are in trouble, burn this incense. I will come at once to aid you," pledged the macaque.

Bujang Permai continued his journey, following the magic bird. After a while he came across a dead firefly. Bujang Permai stopped. He began to recite his magic spells over the dead firefly. Then he whisked it gently with the palm leaf ribs. Yes! The firefly came to life again. "Thank you, Bujang Permai," said the tiny insect. "I want to give you this small gift of incense. If ever you are in need, burn this incense, and I will come at once to aid you."

On another day, Bujang Permai was startled to see a dead squirrel in the path. And when he had revived the squirrel, it too offered incense and a promise to come to his aid should he ever be in need.

An ant too, was found dead. And the ant also pledged his aid.

Bujang Permai was alarmed one day to find his path blocked by a huge dead elephant. Again, he spoke the magic words, then walked around the elephant, whisking it gently with his magic palm leaf ribs. And the elephant too came back to life. "I will come at once if ever you are in need, Bujang Permai," promised the elephant. "Only burn this incense to summon me."

After three long years of wandering in the forest, Bujang Permai came at last to a village on the edge of the next kingdom. There he learned that the brave and courageous king of this land was in great sorrow. His only daughter had been ill for a long time. Many doctors had failed to cure her. The king had sent his ministers throughout the land in search of any doctor who might try.

One day, traveling to seek doctors from afar, one of the ministers happened onto Bujang Permai. Bujang Permai was resting under a tree. Clothed in rags, and dirty from his travels, he looked the part of a beggar lost for years in the forest.

When they had greeted each other, the minister told Bujang Permai of his search. The king had promised that anyone who could cure the princess would have her hand in marriage. Bujang Permai offered to try to cure the princess himself. The chief minister was dubious, seeing Bujang Permai's appearance. But he was desperate, so he agreed to take Bujang Permai to the palace.

As they approached the palace they heard the sounds of people mourning. The beloved Princess Nilam Cahaya had already died. "Bujang Permai, we are too late," moaned the chief minister. You cannot cure the Princess Nilam Cahaya now. She is already dead."

"Do not give up yet," said Bujang Permai. "It is worth a try. Perhaps she can still be cured, if she has just died."

The chief minister took Bujang Permai to the place where the princess was laid out. Even though the king doubted this stranger's ability, he did let Bujang Permai try.

Bujang Permai asked everyone to leave the room of the princess. No one was allowed to see what he was doing.

Bujang Permai took his seven palm leaf ribs. He recited the magic spells learned from the old man. Then he brushed the palm leaf ribs against the body of the princess. Once, twice . . . what happened? Princess Nilam Cahaya awoke! She was alive once more!

But now the princess looked different. Her face was radiant and healthy. Her body seemed lively once again. The princess left her room smiling and beautiful. The king and the queen and all the people of the palace were overjoyed. The mood of the entire palace changed in an instant into one of total joy, now that the princess was well again.

But when the chief minister reminded the king of his promise to take as son-in-law anyone who could cure the princess, the king was not so eager. Bujang Permai looked dirty and the king did not consider him an appropriate match for his daughter.

Looking for a way to avoid this marriage, the king decided to impose a task on Bujang Permai. If he succeeded, he could marry the princess. But the task was to be an impossible one.

"Bujang Permai," ordered the king, "There are a few tasks you must perform before you can wed my daughter. Do you see that small hill in front of us? Level that hill to the ground. I give you one week to finish your task. If you succeed, the wedding will be held."

"I will try, Your Majesty," replied Bujang Permai.

In the night, Bujang Permai burned incense to call the elephant he had helped. In a moment, the elephant arrived. "How can I help you, Bujang Permai?" enquired the huge beast. And when he had heard of the hill that needed to be leveled, the elephant called all of his friends. In a night, the hill was leveled to the ground.

The following day, the king was amazed to see the extent of Bujang Permai's magical powers.

"So, Bujang Permai must not be an ordinary person. He must have divine powers. I will test him again," thought the king.

The king sent for Bujang Permai. "Permai, your task is not done yet. Look at this decayed tree with betel vines entwined throughout it. You must pick all of the betel leaves. But you must not disturb or break the tree in anyway."

Bujang Permai was ready to fulfill the king's order. In the night he burned two kinds of incense, one to call the squirrel, the other to call the macaque. Bujang Permai asked the squirrel to pick all of the leaves from the vine. He asked the macaque to arrange them.

The following morning the people discovered that all the leaves had been picked and arranged in an orderly manner. Again the king was amazed. He thought of another test. The king promised that this would be the last test for Bujang Permai.

Forty beautiful girls were gathered in one room. Among them was the Princess Nilam Cahaya. All forty girls wore the same clothing. The doors and windows were shut and the room was made dark. Now Bujang Permai had to discover the real Princess Nilam Cahaya. If he succeeded, said the king, the wedding party would be prepared.

Many people in the village gathered at the palace. They wanted to see what would happen. Meanwhile Bujang Permai was preparing himself in the palace yard to carry out the king's order. He burned his last bit of incense and called the firefly. Immediately the little firefly appeared before him. He asked the firefly to fly around the room full of girls and try to discover the real princess.

As Bujang Permai moved from girl to girl, the firefly would circle her, checking for the real princess. At last the firefly lit on the nape of one girl's neck. Bujang Permai reached out and took the hand of that girl. Then he called for the light to be brought back into the room. When people could see again, there was Bujang Permai, holding the hand of the Princess Nilam Cahaya.

The king and the entire crowd of people saw clearly that Bujang Permai had accomplished this last task. So a royal wedding party was held. It lasted for seven days and seven nights! All of the people were happy to see their princess healthy and happily married.

Bujang Permai was crowned royal prince and appointed as the king's heir. Thus Bujang Permai had at last achieved his own wish. He had become a king. He ruled with wisdom and dignity.

One day as Bujang Permai was visiting the marketplace to meet with his people, his attention was attracted by someone selling corn. The prince gave the farmer some money and told him to deliver the corn to the palace the next day. Near the man selling corn, Prince Bujang Permai noticed another selling milk. The prince ordered some *dadih* also delivered to his palace the next day.

Early in the morning the corn and *dadih* were delivered. The two men selling the corn and *dadih* were none other than Dahar and Dahir, the brothers of Bujang Permai. The two were surprised to find they had both been called to the palace of the prince at the same time. Bujang Permai had actually recognized the two in the marketplace. But he did not reveal his identity to them.

Bujang Permai asked the brothers about their origin and their parents. Dahar and Dahir told the prince that their parents were still alive. They had been saved by a villager who helped them when the bridge was broken in the flood. They told the prince that there had been three brothers, but their youngest brother was lost to them.

How delighted the prince was to hear that his parents were still living. He gave Dahar and Dahir money to go and fetch their parents. He ordered the building of a large and beautiful house for their parents. He promised to meet them at the new home when they returned. The two brothers were surprised at the kindness of the prince. They did not know the secret behind his order.

After the new house was finished, Bujang Permai left the palace and went to visit the brothers. They politely introduced him to their parents. Still no one recognized this royal prince as Bujang Permai.

After talking for a while, Bujang Permai asked permission to change his clothing. In another room, he took off his princely dress. Then he returned to greet them in simple clothing.

How surprised they all were to see their own son and brother emerge from the room. Dahar and Dahir embraced their youngest brother. He was no longer a youth but had grown into a strong and handsome young man. "Permai! Permai! It is you!" they exclaimed.

His father and mother were very happy to have all of their sons returned to them and to know that Bujang Permai and his brothers had not forgotten them in their old age.

The brothers begged forgiveness of Bujang Permai for treating him so cruelly those many years ago. They explained that they had gone back to rescue him the next day and found him vanished.

"Never mind, brothers," said Bujang Permai. "Let us forget all past things. The most important thing is that all of those wishes we made have been granted. Brother Dahar is a farmer now. Brother Dahir is a breeder of cattle. And I myself have become a king."

And so all of Bujang Permai's family lived happily ever after.

MOLEK

A folktale from Riau Province

A long, long time ago, in a village near a seashore, lived a fisherman and his wife. They had seven beautiful daughters. The youngest daughter was even prettier than her sisters. Her name was Molek. Molek means "beautiful" in the local language.

The beauty of these seven girls was known throughout the village, in neighboring villages, and even in villages and towns located far away. Many young men came to propose marriage to these lovely girls. But none of them met the ideal of the seven beauties. After a while, no young man would dare propose to them. The parents felt ashamed because none of their daughters, who were now grown up girls, had married.

One day it was not a youth who came but a fish, named Jerawan. The fish visited the girls' parents. He asked to marry one of their daughters. As usual the parents conveyed the proposal to their daughters.

First they asked the oldest. She refused. "What? A fish dared to propose marriage to me! How insolent! I'd rather die than become the wife of a disgusting animal. Send him away immediately." The oldest daughter really looked down on the fish.

Since the oldest had refused, the parents offered the proposal to their second Daughter. The second daughter's response was the same. She insulted the gross fish and refused.

The third, fourth, fifth, and sixth daughters all responded in the same way. No one was willing to be wife to a fish.

Eventually the mother asked her youngest daughter, "Molek, I have asked your sisters. Each of them refuses the proposal of Jerawan, the fish. You are the only one I have not asked. Will you marry Jerawan?"

"Mother, although he is an animal, if he is kindhearted and compassionate, and if his attitude is respectful, I will accept his proposal. I will marry the fish, if that is your wish," replied Molek.

"Your father and I will not force you. This must be your own decision. But if you decide to accept the proposal of Jerawan, we will be delighted," answered her mother.

After thinking about this proposal for some time, Molek decided to accept it. She and Jerawan, the fish, were married and lived harmoniously. Every day Molek's sisters mocked her because of her marriage to a disgusting fish. But Molek tried not to be upset by their insults. She did not regret her marriage. In fact she loved her fish husband.

But one thing did disturb Molek. She didn't know where her husband went all day and how he earned his living. Since her sisters always mocked her about her husband's work, Molek determined to follow her husband and find out where he went each day.

One morning when Jerawan left home, Molek secretly followed. She saw him go into the forest. When he reached the middle of the forest, her husband suddenly disappeared into a clump of dense bushes. From a distance she watched. Soon, out of the bushes emerged a handsome young man! Jerawan had taken off his fish skin and hid it under leaves behind the bushes.

Molek almost called out in happiness when she saw her husband emerge from the bushes as a handsome young man. But she calmed herself and followed him quietly. Jerawan strode to the beach, climbed into a sailboat, and gathering a group of fishermen around him, sailed off out to sea. It was clear that Molek's husband owned his own boat and went out on the sea each day as a handsome young fisherman. Only at night, when he returned with his catch and had sold it, did he go back into the forest, put on his fish skin, and come home to his wife . . . as a fish!

Molek kept her husband's secret. She did not say a word to anyone about what she had discovered. Every morning she followed Jerawan into the forest and watched as he changed into the handsome young man. At last she gathered her nerve and developed a plan.

One day when Jerawan had taken off his fish skin and gone to the beach, Molek carefully approached the bushes. There, behind them, she discovered a sprawled heap of fish skin. Molek was frightened by her own actions, but she lifted the fish skin and carried it off to hide it.

That evening when Jerawan returned from his day of fishing, Molek was waiting behind the bushes. Jerawan was shocked when he saw her there in the place where his skin had been left. He turned to run, but Molek grabbed his hand. "My dear husband, don't run away. Please don't cover your handsome appearance with the fish skin again. Let people see who you really are."

"Are you ashamed to be married to a fish?" asked Jerawan.

"No, I am not. Didn't I accept your proposal? Haven't we been happy together all this time? But I have been mocked by my sisters for so long. Does that have to continue? Won't you return home as your true handsome self so they can see that I am married to a fine husband? Then they will stop their mocking. If you really love me, please fulfill this request."

"Very well, if that is what you desire," answered Jerawan. And they started for their home. But Molek asked her husband, "What is your actual name? Jerawan is a fish name. You must have your own human name."

"Yes, my name is Tanara," replied her husband.

"Tanara! Tanara! My dear husband, Tanara. How elegant your name is. Since we have been married you have never told me your real name. At last I know your true name," said Molek happily.

Now their life together was happier. But Molek's sisters became envious and jealous. They regretted not accepting Tanara's proposal. It could have been one of *them* who was married now to the handsome young man. Deep in their hearts, each wanted to attract Tanara and take him away from Molek. Each wanted to become the wife of Tanara.

One day Tanara asked his wife's permission to travel to another island. With a heavy heart, Molek agreed to her husband's plan. Tanara would be at sea for a long time. Molek followed him with her prayers and her hopes for a safe return.

While Tanara was gone, Molek's sisters were happy. They had plotted an evil way to bring misfortune onto their youngest sister. They planned to arrange her death when Tanara returned. Then he would choose one of *them* as his wife.

Several years passed. Then news spread throughout the village that Tanara would soon arrive back home from his journey, bringing a fortune with him. Hearing the news, Molek was happy. She had longed for her husband's return.

On the day of Tanara's arrival, Molek went to the harbor. Pretending to offer kindness, her sisters accompanied her to the shore.

Once they had reached the harbor, Molek's sisters suggested that they should all go out in small boats to await Tanara's arrival. They took two small boats and rowed them out to sea, laughing and splashing water. But when they had rowed far from shore, the sisters suddenly abandoned Molek in one of the boats. "Here, Molek," said the oldest sister. "You can stay here alone in this boat. You don't deserve to have a husband as handsome and elegant as Tanara. It is I who should become his wife. It is wrong for a youngest sister to have this honor."

All of the sisters moved into the other boat, taking the oars with them. "Goodbye, Molek! Wait for your beloved husband *here!*" And they rowed quickly away and back to land, leaving poor Molek stranded at sea.

Poor Molek tried to row the boat using her hands. She prayed that someone would rescue her. But her efforts to paddle the boat with her little hands were in vain. The noon wind rose and began to blow the boat farther out into the open sea. Adrift and buffeted in the small boat, Molek was soon exhausted and in despair. At last she became unconscious.

Meanwhile, in the distance a procession of big ships was seen. They came nearer, loaded with silver, gold, and other precious things. These were the ships of Tanara. At that moment Tanara was on deck enjoying the weather. His view fell on a small boat drifting in the sea. He called to steer the ship closer, and there in the bottom of the boat lay a young girl. "Come," he called to his crew. "This girl is unconscious. Bring her aboard and see if we can aid her."

The crew threw a rope and tied up the small boat, then lifted the girl, carried her onto the ship, and settled her on a bed in the captain's quarters.

Tanara looked at this girl. He was amazed by her beauty. She reminded him of his own wife, Molek. But why would his wife be adrift in a boat?

While Tanara stared in confusion, the girl regained consciousness. Slowly she opened her eyes and with her soft voice she asked, "Where am I? Who brought me to this place? And who are you? Oh! It is you, Tanara! My husband!"

They embraced and began to recount their experiences. When Tanara heard of the sisters abandoning Molek, he was furious. "How mean those sisters are. Leave this to me. I will teach them a lesson for what they did to you."

Tanara had his crewmen bring a large case and hide Molek inside it. Her sisters would not know that she had been rescued.

When he arrived in the harbor, the villagers crowded around to welcome Tanara back from his journey. The people applauded him and swarmed around his ship to see Tanara's wealth. They accompanied him to his house.

Meanwhile Molek's sisters had prepared themselves, waiting for Tanara's homecoming. They dressed beautifully to attract Tanara's heart.

"Where is Molek, my wife? Why isn't she here to greet me?" asked Tanara, pretending not to know.

"We saw her go to the beach. Didn't you meet her there?" asked the sisters, as if they knew nothing about her disappearance.

Tanara looked sad. All the sisters struggled with each other to comfort him and attract him. One served delicious food. Another poured fresh drink. Many of the villagers came to see Tanara, too. A large party was held spontaneously in Tanara's house.

People asked Tanara to tell about his journey. They sat listening entranced while Tanara told of leaving home, of his travels from island to island, of his many adventures and his great wealth.

But just as Tanara was about to end his story with his safe arrival home again, he added, "Unexpectedly, before our ship reached port, a small boat was seen adrift and buffeted in the sea. A helpless girl was in the boat. So we rescued her."

"Where is she now?" cried Molek's six sisters.

"I will introduce her to you. But first, put a chair beside me. She is still very weak."

Tanara's crewmen brought in a beautiful girl. She was as beautiful as an angel. She sat beside Tanara. How equal in beauty they seemed. The young man was handsome and courageous and the girl was lovely beyond compare.

The people who had gathered in Tanara's house looked at the girl carefully. Now they realized that the beautiful girl was actually Molek.

"You witness yourself. This is Molek, my wife, who fell into misfortune. I know already who has done this to her. I do not intend to take revenge on their evil deed. But I hope they feel deep regret for what they have done."

Molek's sisters were ashamed to hear Tanara's remarks. They did regret what they had done and apologized to Molek and Tanara.

Every since that time, Molek and Tanara have lived happily together. They forgave the wicked sisters. And the sisters reformed their ways, let loose their jealousy, and lived in content.

THE THREE BROTHERS

A folktale from Lampung Province

Once upon a time there was a very rich merchant. He had three sons. From childhood on they were spoiled. All their desires had always been granted. Until they grew up they only knew to enjoy their lives.

When the merchant died, his sons had already became adolescents. Because they had no skills and were never taught to help their father, they didn't know how to save money.

Even though they were sad and confused since their father's demise, all they did was eat, drink, and enjoy life.

Gradually the treasure that the merchant had left for his sons was all gone. His sons became poor. All of their money and treasures were gone without a trace.

Now they had to work, nothing more could be eaten or used. So they earned their living by making rice mortars and rice pestles from wood taken from the forest.

One day when they were resting, the eldest said, "I wish for our lives to become contented again like it used to be." His youngest brother said, "When I grow up, I want to sit on a golden chair with a diamond throne and in front of me spread out a beautiful carpet."

Listening to their youngest brother's wish, the eldest became angry. He considered that his brother's ideals were too high and didn't make any sense.

Therefore the two older brothers hated their youngest brother. They hated him so much that they cast him off in the middle of the forest.

After he was discarded, Youngest now lived alone in the forest. He could eat nothing except the leaves. For his bed, Youngest climbed a tree.

Under that tree a herd of wild boars used to wallow in the mud. When they came, Youngest quickly climbed the tree and hid among the leaves in order not to be seen.

One day a herd of wild boars came to wallow as usual. In the distance noisy voices were heard. Quickly Youngest hid behind the leaves.

From high in the tree, he saw the king of the wild boars take off a necklace that hung on his neck and hook it on a small branch of the tree where Youngest was hiding.

Youngest was very curious to see the necklace. Slowly he reached for the necklace and hid it in his pocket.

After the boars were satisfied with wallowing they left Youngest's hiding place. Apparently the king of the boars had forgotten his necklace.

How happy Youngest was to get the beautiful necklace. But he didn't know that the necklace he had taken was a magic necklace. Whoever wore it would be able to float on water.

One day Youngest went to bathe in the sea. At first he was just bathing on the edge, but bit by bit his courage rose to go farther into the deeper part of the sea. He felt his body become lighter and lighter. Finally he could walk on the sea surface.

The following day he decided to cross the sea to go to a foreign country.

Early in the morning he left the place where he had been hiding all this time. He had not forgotten to wear the magic necklace. Arriving in the foreign country, Youngest wondered at the beauty of the city. All day long he just walked with no destination.

When evening came, he stopped by one of the villager's houses. He asked permission to take a rest.

The owner of the house wanted to know his circumstances. With sadness Youngest told his story from the beginning. The owner took pity on Youngest and invited him to stay with him.

Youngest was very diligent in helping his landlord. Early in the morning he woke up. Afterward he boiled water, cooked the rice, and cleaned up the house. His landlord was happy to see Youngest's good behavior.

One day Youngest's landlord went to the palace and reported to the king that there was a youth who lived with him.

He said that the youth was very industrious, could be trusted, and behaved well. Listening to this report the king ordered Youngest to appear before him.

When Youngest appeared, the king had a sense Youngest was a good person, diligent and reliable.

So he commanded Youngest to work in the palace to help the palace workers. How happy Youngest was to be able to live in the palace. He was very grateful to his former landlord.

Days passed by. Months and years passed by. Now Youngest was an adolescent. He looked handsome and was capable of doing any job he was in charge of. Therefore the king intended to marry Youngest to his only daughter.

The princess agreed with her father's intention, so a royal wedding party was held for the princess and Youngest. The king ordered the slaughter of seven water buffaloes and the wedding party was held for seven days and seven nights. The party was carried out merrily. All the people of the kingdom came to celebrate.

Several years later, the king felt that he was already old and wanted to take a rest. He gave his kingdom to his daughter and Youngest. It happened thus that Youngest became a king. His wish had been fulfilled.

Now he became a king, sitting on a golden chair with a diamond throne and in front of him spread out a thick and beautiful carpet. Youngest ruled wisely and fairly. He was very respected by his people.

Years passed by, and news was heard that two men who were selling rice mortars and rice pestles had come to his kingdom. Youngest remembered his two brothers, so he sent his soldier to summon the two merchants to come to the palace.

Even though his brothers had done an evil thing to him, Youngest didn't bear a grudge. He hoped to be able to meet his two brothers again.

On receiving the king's command, his two brothers were startled and frightened. They thought they would be punished because they had entered the kingdom. With fear and wonder they appeared before the king.

When they arrived in the palace, Youngest immediately recognized them as his brothers. But his brothers didn't know that the king who sat in front of them was Youngest.

Youngest asked, "Do you recognize me?" His two brothers didn't dare look at the king at first. Then they answered him while gazing at him, "Forgive me Your Majesty, we don't recognize you."

His two brothers could not identify their brother because Youngest had become more handsome and wore the royal costume.

Youngest then said, "Do you remember a boy who wanted to sit on a golden chair with a diamond throne and a thick and beautiful carpet in front of him?"

How startled his two brothers were. They remembered when they cast off their brother in the middle of the wood. They thought that this brother had been eaten by wild animals.

The two brothers then paid homage, asking for forgiveness for their mistakes and hatred. Youngest, who was kindhearted, forgave his brothers. They hugged and wept for each other because they had met again.

Youngest then asked his brothers to live with him as palace employees. They lived in harmony ever after.

Stories of Independent Princesses

The most common goal for women characters in folktales seems to be to become rich and marry a prince. This was a way for a common girl to raise her social status. However, Princess Pinang Masak chose to escape marriage to an unsavory older king. Princess White Hair also chose to live singly rather than accept marriage. These two stories present an unusual model of a strong, independent princess able to stand on her own two feet. Princess Kemang is one of the few stories in which a woman proposes marriage to the prince. It is unusual also in that it portrays a woman who has chosen for herself the pursuits of a man.

PRINCESS WHITE HAIR

A folktale from Perigi Village in South Sumatera Province

Long, long ago there lived a very beautiful young girl. Her beauty was known throughout the kingdom. Not only was she beautiful, but people said that her saliva had a magical power.

Hearing about her beauty, many young men and princes came to the girl's village to propose marriage to her. But none were well received. Not only would she reject them, but she would also spit onto their heads. Her magic spit turned their hair white! Because of this people called the arrogant young girl Princess White Hair.

The king heard of the beauty of Princess White Hair. He resolved to marry her himself and sent his chief commander to extend his proposal of marriage.

Princess White Hair just spit on the head of the chief commander and sent him back to the king with a head of white hair!

The king was very embarrassed. Soon he sent another chief commander to the village of Princess White Hair to try to discover the reasons for her strange behavior and arrogant attitude. The king was planning to kidnap the princess.

Secretly the chief commander went to Perigi village where Princess White Hair lived. No one knew that he was the chief commander. Living quietly in the village, he began to investigate this Princess White Hair.

He learned that the young girl had a brother. His name was Langkusa. He lived as a hermit and had mastered mysticism. No one could defeat him because of his divine power. Because of this, Princess White Hair had become very arrogant.

The chief commander reported to the king about Langkusa's divine power. The king was surprised, but he didn't give up. He would find a way to kill Langkusa.

The king heard about a fierce bull that lived in the forest. When this bull smelled human blood he would become drunk and chase his prey until he had killed it.

Thinking that he could arrange the death of Langkusa in this way, the king went with his chief commanders to visit Perigi village. Langkusa was in meditation when the king arrived. The king send his chief commander to summon Langkusa, who left his meditation and came at once before the king.

"Your Majesty, why do you come to this village? What do you decree?"

"Langkusa, the people report that they are disturbed by a fierce wild bull. Find and catch the beast," commanded the king.

"Yes, Your Majesty," answered Langkusa, "I will leave at once."

Langkusa went into the woods to find the wild bull. From a distance the beast had already smelled a human. It raged violently and made a thundering sound like a hurricane. Then it began to stampede in the direction of Langkusa.

Langkusa squared off for a fight with the furious bull. He was ready to face this danger. When the bull attacked, he nimbly parried it. The bewildered bull attacked him time and again, but Langkusa dodged away and the bull was unable to gore him. Becoming more and more ferocious, the bull continued to attack. But when at last it did succeed in hitting the magical Langkusa, the bull's head smashed to pieces and the bull died instantly.

Langkusa carried the dead bull to the village and presented its body to the king. "Your Majesty, here is the bull that disturbed the people. I have fulfilled my duty to you."

When the king saw that Langkusa had succeeded in killing the wild bull, he thought of another way to bring about his death. He sent his servants to put spears on the bottom of the village well with the blades sticking up, then he called Langkusa.

"I have one more request, Langkusa. My ring has fallen accidentally into the village well. I need your help to recover it."

Langkusa knew that the sharp spears had been put into the well, but he didn't hesitate to accept the king's order.

"Yes, Your Majesty. Your servant will do as you command."

Langkusa jumped into the well. The sound of spears hitting Langkusa's body could be clearly heard. But protected by his magic, Langkusa's body was unharmed. Instead all of the spears were snapped off and broken.

Langkusa climbed out of the well and handed the ring back to the king.

The king had failed to kill Langkusa. He and his chief commanders returned to the palace. But the king did not give up. He gathered his soldiers and asked them, "Which one of you dares kidnap Princess White Hair for me?" No one answered. It was deathly quiet in the room.

"Very well," said the king. "Then you are all assigned to work on the excavation of a new river. The river will reach to the home of Princess White Hair." The soldiers were put to work digging, and when their long, hard task was finished, water flowed into the newly dug river.

Now the king and his soldiers set sail up their new river. Upon arrival at the upper reaches of the river, the king descended from his boat and walked to the home of Princess White Hair.

Princess White Hair was making clay cooking pots at her home. Langkusa was off bathing in the river. Seeing that she was alone and unprotected, the king ordered his soldiers to grab her and carry her to his boat. There she was hidden in the king's chamber, and the boat set off with her.

A villager had seen the kidnapping take place and hurried to alert her brother. "Langkusa, your sister has been kidnapped by the king. Hurry to rescue her!"

"Don't worry. Go on back home. I will finish my bathing first," answered Langkusa.

Langkusa kept calmly bathing in the river.

Another villager hurried to warn him, "Langkusa, your sister has been kidnapped by the king. Hurry and rescue her!"

"I am bathing just now. Go on back home. I will rescue her when I am finished."

A third time, a villager went to urge Langkusa to go after his sister.

"All right, I am finished bathing now. Where did you say she was taken?"

"The king has kidnapped her and carried her away on his boat!"

"Don't worry. Go on home. I will bring her back."

Langkusa took one huge jump. In only one leap he reached the shore beside the king's boat. "Your Majesty, I am going to jump into your boat. Please balance your boat."

"Go ahead," replied the king. "My boat is big. It will not sink."

Langkusa made a very quick jump, grabbed his sister, and leaped away again.

Astonished, the king and his soldiers didn't think to balance their boat. They just stared in alarm at Langkusa, not realizing their ship was about to overturn.

Before the king and his soldiers could do anything to stop him, Langkusa had taken his sister under his arm, jumped to the shore, and raced off home. In their haste, the hairpin of the princess fell into the river.

The disappointed king returned to his palace. His anger was so great that he cursed the entire Perigi village. "From this moment, not one of my offspring is allowed to marry into the Kayu Agung family at Perigi village. Anyone who goes against my curse will suffer."

Thus the conceited Princess White Hair remained unmarried all of her life. No man dared propose marriage to her. Not that the arrogant princess ever showed any intention of wanting to be married!

In Perigi Village people say that the deep Lubuk Tangubai pool in the river near there was caused by the pin (tangubai) of Princess White Hair falling into the river when she leaped with her brother from the king's ship.

PRINCESS PINANG MASAK

A folktale from Senuro Village in South Sumatera Province

Once upon a time there was a beautiful girl. Her name was Napisah, but she was also called Princess Pinang Masak. In the local language *pinang masak* means ripe areca nut. Perhaps she was as beautiful as a ripe areca nut to the people of her village.

This beautiful young girl lived in a small village in a kingdom. The king was known to be fond of bringing young, beautiful girls to his court and keeping them there for his own pleasure.

The king had heard that in this small village there lived a beauty named Princess Pinang Masak. Her beauty was said to be unmatched throughout the whole kingdom. It was the talk of the entire kingdom, and many young men had already competed to marry her.

The king wanted to know the truth of this matter, so he ordered several of his chief commanders to take this Princess Pinang Masak and bring her to his palace.

When Princess Pinang Masak heard of the king's intention, she was distressed. She decided she would rather die than join the many young women held prisoner at the king's palace. She sought a way to avoid being taken there, but she knew it would be hard to escape the king's vicious soldiers.

Then she thought of a plan. Princess Pinang Masak boiled deep purple banana blossoms until she had a vat of dark liquid, then bathed in the maroon-colored banana blossom water. As she covered herself in this dark liquid, her skin began to look streaked and dirty. Her beauty was disguised and ruined. Then she put on the oldest rags she could find and waited for the king's soldiers to arrive.

When the soldiers came to take her to the palace, they found no beauty but only a dirty looking, unsightly girl in rags. They could not believe the king wanted this creature, but they took her to the palace as commanded.

When they brought her to the king, he was horrified and disgusted that such an unsightly girl should be brought before him. Immediately he expelled Princess Pinang Masak from his palace and harshly sent her back to her village.

However, her misfortune did not end with that. Young men continued to arrive at her village proposing marriage, for the fame of her beauty was still known far and wide.

News of the princess continuing to receive suitors reached the king. He wondered if he had been deceived in some way and sent soldiers to investigate. When they reported that Princess Pinang Masak was indeed very beautiful, he ordered her captured and brought once more to the palace.

But Princess Pinang Masak had heard of the king's intentions. She called together four faithful friends and two guards, and they planned her escape. Leaving by night, the seven sailed along the rivers and lowlands looking for a new place to avoid the pursuit of the soldiers.

Their boat passed a wide lowland, which was later called Lebak (lowland) Maranjat, and a bay (*teluk*) called Teluk Lancang. Before long they sailed through a swamp that had a fast current.

Traveling far, they at last discovered a safe, hidden place to reside and settled down there. The people nearby welcomed Princess Pinang Masak. Living here, the princess changed her name and took the name Princess Senuro. Gradually the place grew into a village and was named Senuro village after the lovely princess.

In this new place, Princess Senuro was still the young men's ideal. She taught basketry skills and instructed in the making of plaited materials such as baskets and other kitchen utensils. It was said that she could plait a basket so well that it could not be penetrated by water.

Years passed. One day Princess Senuro fell ill. With time her sickness became worse and worse. Before she died she swore an oath. "I beg God Almighty that my descendants should not be as beautiful as I am. Beauty can cause calamities such as have befallen me."

After she spoke this oath, she breathed her last. She left her four faithful friends and two brave guards who had protected her until her death. Her four friends and two guards remained living in this village until they too died and were buried beside the grave of Princess Senuro.

For the people in that village, Princess Senuro is a symbol of women who hold in high esteem the dignity of women.

As for Princess Senuro's oath, people say that since that time the girls in Senuro village are less beautiful than girls from other villages.

PRINCESS KEMANG

A folktale from Bengkulu

There was once a kingdom in the outskirts of a dense forest. The king had a daughter who was very like a man in her nature. She was fond of hunting, fishing, and hiking in the woods. Therefore Princess Kemang had been called up to serve as a soldier in the army. She mastered sword fighting. She was excellent with the bow and arrow, and she handled a spear as well as any man.

One day Princess Kemang went hunting for deer. She carried her sword and her spear. Her beloved dog came with her. The princess walked from one woods to another, from one forest to another, from one meadow to another, and from one hill to another. She rafted across many rivers and swam across others.

Eventually, after a long journey, Princess Kemang spotted a striped-leg deer. She shot her arrow quickly but missed. Angry at this, she chased after the deer. Wherever it ran, she was right behind. Never for a minute did she take her eyes off the deer.

The deer ran deep into the woods. Then suddenly it stopped under a kemang tree. This is the wild mango tree for which Princess Kemang was named. As Princess Kemang came near, she realized that the tree was calling to her. "Dear Princess, don't chase after this deer. This deer is actually a tiger in disguise."

Princess Kemang was startled to hear the kemang tree give her this advice. But she was determined to kill the deer. Climbing the kemang tree, she shot her arrow straight through the body of the deer. At the instant it died, the deer transformed into a tiger. Leaping down from the tree, Princess Kemang began to skin the tiger.

But just then something even stranger happened. The kemang tree moved and slowly changed itself into a handsome young man.

"Who are you? How can you change your form like this?" exclaimed the princess.

"I am the guardian of this forest," answered the handsome young man.

"Come with me and we will hunt together," she pleaded.

"But I can't leave the forest until every thing in the forest has changed into its human form and the forest has turned into a kingdom," replied the young man.

"I agree," replied the princess. "I promise that if the forest becomes a kingdom, I will return for you. I want to be your friend."

After uttering these words, the princess continued her hunt, leaving the handsome man standing guard in the forest.

Some time later, Princess Kemang met a cat. The princess's dog barked fiercely. But instead of running away, the cat began to grow. The dog barked even more ferociously. But the cat grew even bigger. And then suddenly it pounced on the dog and swallowed it!

Princess Kemang was distraught at the loss of her dear dog. She sadly turned to go back home. The princess walked alone now, as her dear dog was dead. But when she came to the river, it was infested with crocodiles and she could not cross. The crocs looked very hungry.

The biggest crocodile spoke to her. "Princess, now your life too comes to an end. You will be our meal."

The princess replied, "Crocodile, I understand that you are the biggest and strongest animal. But I am sure you are not capable of fighting me alone. I can fight a thousand crocodiles myself."

"Really? I want to see this. Let me call my friends. We will see if you can fight one thousand of us!" replied the angry crocodile.

"All right. You crocodiles line up, so I can count you. I want to make sure there are really one thousand before the battle begins."

So the crocodiles came and formed a line. There were so many crocodiles that they stretched from one side of the river to the other. Princess Kemang quickly jumped onto the back of the first crocodile. "This is one." She called. "This is two," she jumped to the back of the second crocodile. "Three . . . four . . . five . . . six. . . ." And jumping from back to back as she counted, the princess easily crossed the wide river. Before she reached a thousand she had reached the other side. She jumped ashore and called out loudly, "Thank you, stupid crocodiles! You are too greedy. How could you feed yourselves with just my small meat anyway? Look for another meal. There are a lot of rivers on the earth."

How angry the crocodiles were. They realized their stupidity.

When Princess Kemang arrived at the palace, she told the king and the queen all the experiences of her journey.

A year later, Princess Kemang was out hunting again. She found herself in a huge woods and walked along a long river there. After three days she came upon a large kingdom. Princess Kemang was very surprised to see a kingdom here in the forest. She met an old man and asked him, "What is the name of this kingdom, Old Man? And who is the king here?"

"This is Kemang Kingdom. Prince Kemang is the king. Before, this was a dense forest. It was called ghost forest, because the entire forest was occupied by supernatural spirits. Prince Kemang was a god who had been cursed by the gods in heaven. He became a large kemang tree, which grew in the middle of the forest. The gods' curse said that whenever a human would speak to the tree, it would change into a human again and the forest could become a kingdom."

Princess Kemang remembered her experiences in her past journey in this forest. She said to the old man, "Old Man, please take me to Prince Kemang."

Accompanied by the old man, Princess Kemang went to the palace. When they met, Prince Kemang said, "Dear Princess, you are the hunter who met me last year, aren't you?"

"Yes, it is I," answered the princess. "I come to fulfill my promise to fetch you after you became a human."

They promised to become friends. After a few days, Princess Kemang invited Prince Kemang to visit her kingdom. So they traveled together. Their journey took five long days.

Before dawn on the fifth day, they arrived at the kingdom of Princess Kemang. The king approached them with happiness. He welcomed the prince with food and drinks and asked about his origin.

The king was very surprised to hear the prince's story. He asked the prince to become his son-in-law. So the servants were commanded to prepare a royal wedding party. It was celebrated for seven days and seven nights.

When the king became old, he gave his throne to his daughter. The two kingdoms were united into a large and victorious kingdom. And they lived happily ever after.

Stories of Ungrateful Children

Indonesians are taught to be grateful and obedient, to respect their parents from childhood on, to love their parents, and to appreciate their parent's exertions. Stories of ungrateful children are found in all cultures in Indonesia. The most famous one is *The Legend of Malin Kundang* from West Sumatera Province, which is passed from generation to generation all over the country. People in Indonesia believe that parents' blessings and prayers will help children to live safe and happy lives.

It is interesting to note that most of the characters in these stories are boys. Stories with girl characters are rare. *Rawa Tekuluk*, from West Sumatera Province, has a girl as the main character. In the ungrateful children stories rebelliousness toward the mother will be punished. It is rare to find stories that teach parents not to neglect their children.

THE LEGEND OF MALIN KUNDANG

A folktale from West Sumatera Province

Near the town of Padang, in the mouth of the Batang Arau River in West Sumatera, we see a heap of rocks. People say the rocks are the remains of the ship of Malin Kundang, a son who was unkind to his mother. This is their story.

Near the mouth of the Batang Arau River there once was a large fishing village. Its harbor was crowded with large ships and sailing vessels from all corners of the world.

Among the many fishing families, there lived a poor fisherman and his wife and son. Their only child was so spoiled that he was called Malin *Kundang*. Malin was the boy's name, but "Kundang" meant "spoiled."

Malin Kundang was a naughty child. One day when he was playing too roughly, he fell and wounded his forehead. It left a scar that clearly marked the boy. Even when he was grown into a young man, the scar could plainly be seen.

When Malin Kundang was a young man, he was so well built and strong that his father was able to secure a place for him with a sea captain. "Dear sir, if you need a crewman, please take my son with you. You may bring him up and consider him your own son. I hope he can learn much from you, sir, and perhaps one day become a captain like yourself."

The ship's captain was willing to take Malin Kundang aboard, and Malin Kundang was excited by the opportunity to see other countries.

It was hard for Malin Kundang's parents to see him off at the port. They watched until the ship disappeared from sight. Then they returned to their little hut, only hoping that they one day would see their beloved son again.

Day after day, week after week, year after year passed. Malin Kundang worked diligently and learned a great deal. He made a fortune for himself. He became a sea captain, with a large, luxurious ship of his own. He married the daughter of a wealthy merchant. And he completely forgot his own native village and his loving parents who still waited for his return.

Years passed and his parents grew older and older. His father died, but his old mother still waited, hoping to see her son once more.

Eventually Malin Kundang did begin to think of his native village. He decided to make a trip to visit the scenes of his childhood. He had never told his wife of his origins for fear she would spurn one of such lowly birth.

When his grandiose ship arrived in the harbor of Batang Arau the villagers all rushed to see the wonderful sight. Who could be the owner of the luxurious vessel?

Then one old man in the crowd spied the scar on the forehead of the ship's captain. It could only be Malin Kundang. He hurried to tell Malin Kundang's mother that her son had arrived as a rich merchant. How happy she was to hear the news of her son's homecoming after all these years.

Before long the news had spread throughout the entire village. But keeping her longing to herself for a while more, Malin Kundang's mother quickly prepared Malin Kundang's favorite food. Then she and her neighbor hurried to the port to greet her son.

There was the marvelous ship, and on its deck a most handsome man in such expensive clothing. Malin Kundang's mother was so proud to see her son's accomplishment.

Arriving near the ship, she called out, "Malin Kundang! My dear son! At last you have come home! Malin Kundang, my son! I have been longing and waiting for you all these years. Here is your mother, dear son!" She was full of happiness, for she had seen the scar on the rich merchant's forehead and knew that this really was her own son.

But when Malin Kundang saw this old woman in poor clothing calling to him, he was too ashamed to answer. Turning away, he ordered his crewmen to remove her from the shore.

"But Malin Kundang," called his mother. "Just look at me. You must recognize your own mother. I am bringing your favorite food. Remember when you were a child?

"How I have longed for your return, my son." She held up the food. But Malin Kundang still turned away. He would not admit before his wife and crewmen that this poor old woman was his own mother.

Still his mother called out to him, "Malin Kundang, how can you forget me? I am your own mother! Look at me carefully, Malin Kundang! You must have missed me."

Malin Kundang was ashamed. With no compassion whatsoever, he told her, "Shameless old woman. I do not have a dirty and poor mother like this. My mother is dead. Don't ever claim yourself as my mother." And his crewmen dragged her off.

His broken hearted mother could only call after him, "Malin Kundang, you are a wicked child! You neglect your own mother. You are an ungrateful child, ashamed to admit your own mother who brought you up." She went home in sorrow, with a broken heart.

The following day, Malin Kundang ordered his crew to weigh anchor and set sail from his native village. But once they reached the middle of the sea, the wind rose and began to hurl Malin Kundang's ship left and right. Lightning and thunder took over the sky. The clouds were pitch dark. The sounds were deafening.

Malin Kundang realized his sin toward his mother. He knew that God and nature were conspiring to punish him for his contemptible deed. He began to pray and cry for forgiveness. But it was too late. The waves became more and more fierce. At last his ship was swallowed by a wave and it sank from sight.

They say that the wreckage of Malin Kundang's ship was cast ashore near Air Manis, near the city of Padang. There it was turned into stones, a reminder of the wickedness of those who refuse to acknowledge their own parents. You can see the stones to this day on the shore near Air Manis. People interpret the shapes of the remaining stones as the cursed Maling Kundang and his wrecked ship.

Artificial ruins built by the local authority represent Malin Kundang and the wreckage of his ship. The original stones can be seen on the shore near Air Manis, near the city of Padang. Photograph by Untung Safroni.

THE SPOILED LITTLE KITTEN

A folktale from Deli Serdang in North Sumatera Province

Long, long ago there lived a king who was fair and wise. He was loved by all his people. They lived sufficiently in a prosperous and peaceful kingdom. But this king had no heir.

As companions, the king kept many animals in his palace. These cheered him up considerably. But of all his animals, the king loved most his Siamese cat. So when the Siamese cat had a kitten, that kitten was completely spoiled.

One day the palace caught fire. The Siamese cat and her kitten just managed to escape into the forest. But now their life was much different than it had been at the palace. Instead of having food served to them daily on a golden platter, the mother cat now had to search everywhere for food for herself and her kitten. And instead of helping his mother, the kitten still chose to lie about waiting to be fed on a golden platter.

The poor mother cat worked hard to bring food to her kitten, but she began to suffer from the work. Though her son was no longer a baby, still she had to go out each day and find his food for him.

Seeing what a pitiful state his mother had arrived at, the son no longer considered her a suitable provider. "I will go find myself a better mother," he decided. "I need a mother who can feed me on a golden platter as I deserve."

So the spoiled kitten set off to find a better mother.

Soon he noticed the sun's heat and an idea occurred to him. "If the sun were my mother, my life would be very contented," he thought. So he went to the sun.

"Dear Sun, would you be my mother? I want to enjoy a pleasant life like yours."

But Sun replied, "My life is pleasant. But the mist obscures me whenever it wants. The mist can make my life quite unpleasant."

"Then I want Mist for my mother," said the spoiled kitten. And he hurried off to find Mist.

"Dear Mist, would you be my mother? I want to enjoy a pleasant life like yours."

"It is true, that my life is superior to that of the sun," said Mist. "But the Wind can cause me great trouble, blowing me wherever it wants. When Wind attacks me, I am blown into pieces and end by becoming mere drops of water."

"Then Wind should be my mother!" said the spoiled kitten. And off he went to seek Wind.

"Dear Wind, would you be my mother? I want to enjoy a pleasant life like yours."

"My life is pleasant enough," said Wind. "But Hill causes me great injury. Whenever I meet a hill, I am stopped in my tracks and cannot continue my journey."

"Then I want Hill for my mother," said the spoiled kitten.

"Dear Hill, would you be my mother? I want to have a pleasant life like yours."

"My life is pleasant some of the time," replied Hill. "But Carabao gives me great pain. She butts and stamps my body until I am ruined and sometimes even leveled to the ground. Carabao has a better life than mine."

"Then I want Carabao for my mother," said the spoiled kitten. And he went to ask Carabao.

"Dear Carabao, Would you be my mother? I want to live a pleasant life like yours."

"Well, my life is pleasant most of the time," said Carabao. "But Rattan makes my life miserable. Rattan ties me up until I cannot move."

"Oh my, I don't want *you* for my mother. I will ask Rattan." And the spoiled kitten went to Rattan.

"Dear Rattan, Carabao says you can tie him up. You must be superior to Carabao. I want to live a happy life. Would you be my mother?"

"I do have a happy life," said Rattan. "But I fear Rat. Rat is my enemy. When Rat bites me the pain is unbearable. And I can be bitten into bits by that small animal."

"Then I certainly don't want *you* for my mother," said the spoiled kitten. "I want Rat!"

"Dear Rat, would you be my mother? I want a mother who can keep me in comfort. Sun is annoyed by Mist. Mist is scattered by Wind. Wind is blocked by Hill. Hill is trampled by Carabao. Carabao is tied by Rattan. Rattan is gnawed to bits by Rat. You, Rat are superior. You can provide me with a life of comfort such as I wish."

"All this is true," said Rat. "Yet there is one who makes my life miserable too. In this forest there lives a thin old cat. She tracks my every move. One day she will catch me and I will die."

Suddenly the spoiled kitten realized just who the thin, old cat must be.

"Do you mean the old cat who lives alone in the middle of the woods?"

"Exactly. That is the old cat I fear," replied the rat.

"But that is my *own* mother!" cried the spoiled kitten.

And rushing home, he begged his mother's forgiveness and settled down to be a good son. He realized now that if he was to find happiness, it must be with his own mother.

Fortunately the kitten now lost his spoiled ways and became a diligent and obedient child. Now that there were two of them to share the work, he and his mother lived a happy and comfortable life in their forest home.

SIKINTAN

A folktale from Jamu Region in Aceh Province

In a village there lived a family with only one son. His name was Sikintan. Every day the father went into the forest to gather wood, which he sold in the market. Though he worked hard, they were always poor.

One night Sikintan's father had a dream. In his dream an old man came to him and said, "Sikintan's father, go to the upper reaches of the river. Look there for a large bamboo cluster. In that bamboo cluster you will find a diamond stick. That diamond stick will bring much good fortune."

The following day Sikintan was asked by his father to come along on a trip to the upper reaches of the river. But his father didn't tell Sikintan what his exact purpose was. His father only told him they were going for a long walk.

Father and son walked along the edge of the river. When they had traveled far upstream to the very upper reaches of the river, they discovered a large bamboo cluster. Sikintan was astonished to see his father start digging furiously in the bamboo cluster. But still his father did not tell him what he was actually looking for.

After a while, something sparkling was seen among the bamboo roots. Sikintan's father soon pried it up from the thick bamboo clump. It was the diamond stick that had been revealed by the old man in the dream. Not until he actually had the diamond stick in his hands did the father tell Sikintan about that dream.

When they arrived home, Sikintan's mother was amazed to see her husband carrying a diamond stick! They decided they should sell it and use the money to forward Sikintan's career, since he was now old enough to go out into the world. But since everyone on their island knew them as poor people, they feared they would be accused of stealing if they tried to sell something so valuable. They decided to send Sikintan to another island to make the sale.

The following day Sikintan hired himself onto a large boat traveling to another island . "You will soon be rich, my son," said his father. "Don't forget your poor parents who have always lived in poverty. Remember us when your life improves." Sikintan promised to always remember his parents.

So Sikintan crossed the seas to a distant island. As soon as the ship had moored, Sikintan went ashore and looked for work. He settled down to learn his way about before attempting to sell the diamond stick. He soon realized that only the most wealthy merchant in the village would have enough money to purchase such a thing. So he approached that merchant and managed to sell the marvelous diamond stick for a large sum.

With the money from the diamond stick, Sikintan set himself up as a merchant. He used his money well, worked hard, and became very rich. He married a merchant's daughter, built a fine house, and bought for himself a large ship, which he named *Sikintan*. But all this time he had not thought at all about his parents, still living in his home village in such poverty.

Then one night Sikintan had a dream. In his dream he saw his mother and father. "Kintan," called his mother, "You are now rich and contented. But you seem to have forgotten your parents. We have been waiting for you for so many years. Did you not promise your father when he saw you off at the ship, that you would never forget your own parents?"

Sikintan realized his shameful neglect of his parents. The next day he and his wife set sail for his native village. As soon as he docked, he sent word for his parents to come to the ship. News spread throughout the village that Sikintan had returned a rich merchant.

Sikintan's father was overjoyed and rushed to the shore to greet his son. But when Sikintan saw this old man in ragged clothes on the shore, he was ashamed to admit before his wife that this was his own father.

"Old man, how do you dare claim to be my father? My father is not a poor old creature like you." Sikintan's father tried to be patient. "Kintan, look at me carefully. I am your father. It was I who gave you the diamond stick that made your fortune. It is because of me that you now can live in such wealth, while your old parents have lived in poverty all of these years."

But Sikintan turned his back on the ragged old man. His father went home in grief.

"Though Sikintan sent for me, he refused to recognize me when I arrived," he told his wife. "You must go to call him. Surely he will recognize his own mother."

So Sikintan's mother hurried to the ship and asked someone to call Sikintan to the deck. But when he came out onto the deck and saw this old, decrepit woman, he once more refused to show recognition. "Old woman, don't you ever claim me as your son. My mother didn't look like you. My mother was always neatly dressed and clean."

"But Kintan," replied his mother. I am old now, and we are very poor. How can you show shame at meeting your own parents?"

So his mother too had to go home griefstricken. There she and her husband wept and wept that their own son would refuse to recognize them.

As for Sikintan, he turned his ship and started back for the village of his wife. But soon the wind began to blow. The ship's captain was alarmed. "Sikintan has been cruel to his own parents. This typhoon may be a retribution for his actions. Now we will all suffer because of Sikintan."

Sikintan realized that the captain was right. Fearing for his life, he ordered the captain to change course and return to his parent's island. Once more the huge ship docked at his parent's village. Once more they hurried to the shore to greet their son. But when he saw that old, ragged couple on the shore, Sikintan still could not bear to admit that they were his own parents. So happy at first, his parents now were crushed once again. "If you still do not want to recognize us, we will just go home. Forget you ever had us as your parents." And they left.

As Sikintan's ship sailed away a final time, his mother called to the heavens. "Since our son, Sikintan, does not admit we are his parents, let him have no blessing from us or from the heavens."

Now the typhoon arose again. This time there was no turning back. The ship was swallowed in the waves, and Sikintan, his wife, and all his crew were drowned.

They say that seven days after the ship sank, an island appeared on that spot. A white monkey clung to the island. For one month the white monkey was seen clinging there, then it was gone. People say that the island was Sikintan's ship and that the white monkey was Sikintan himself. To this day that island is known as Sikintan's Island. And all who pass it remember the story of Sikintan who treated his own parents so cruelly.

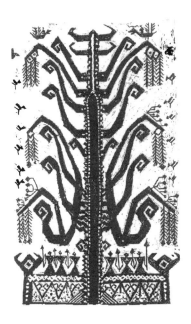

Sikintan

RAWA TEKULUK

A folktale from West Sumatera Province

There was once a family who lived with their daughter, named Upik. She was very spoiled. Upik's father and mother loved her very much and never taught her to help with their work in the farm. Besides, she didn't want to help her mother in cooking, washing, or cleaning the house. Upik became a lazy person who was awkward at work.

After some time, Upik's father died. Their life became miserable.

Their small piece of rice field could not help to improve their life's condition. Moreover, it was only the mother who worked hard to feed the family. Upik couldn't be expected to help her mother.

One day the harvest in the entire village failed. Life became more difficult. The villagers called it a period of starving.

But conditions in the neighboring village were better. The name of the village was *Bukit Kecil* (small hill). Upik's mother went to that village to help the neighbors work in the rice field and for this she got a small wage. With this Upik's mother could meet the needs of the daily life modestly.

In the village of *Bukit Kecil*, every morning the wage earners got something to drink. But at lunch and in the evening they got various dishes. Therefore Upik's mother told her daughter to come with her, not to help her at work but to share with her the food she received. She only ate a small piece and gave Upik the biggest part. But when her mother was working, Upik just sat and watched her. She had no intention of helping to lighten her mother's burden even a bit.

After working for a few days, the work in *Bukit Kecil* was done. On the last day, Upik's mother received fifteen *sukat*s of rice as her pay (one *sukat* is 27.5 lbs or 12.5 kg). At first Upik's mother tried to carry it by herself. But being old, she could only carry it to a nearby swamp, not far from the place she had worked.

There they stopped and Upik's mother said, "Upik, I divide this rice into two parts. You bring five *sukat*s and I will bring the remaining ten *sukat*s by myself."

"I am not able to bring it, Mother! I am not used to work. Bring all the rice by yourself," replied Upik. In the meantime the night came.

Even though Upik refused to help, the mother divided the rice into two parts. She brought the ten *sukat*s of rice in that day and she hid the remaining five *sukat*s under the bushes so that nobody saw it. Then they went home.

The following day it was clear weather and burning heat, a good day to dry the rice. The rice had to be dried first, so that it could be made into hulled rice as quickly as possible.

This task was very strenuous because the rice had to be carried from the house to the yard and also had to be stirred up frequently so that the grains would get heat evenly.

Upik couldn't help because from childhood on she had never done anything.

The drying of the rice needed constant attention, so Upik's mother could not leave this work. Therefore she told Upik to go get the remaining rice she had hidden near the swamp the evening before.

This time her mother forced Upik to go.

Nagging and grumbling, hurriedly Upik went to the swamp. She said to her mother, "Why did you leave the five *sukat*s of rice? Now it is I who have to suffer from the heat of the sun and toil to get them." After a while she was back home without the rice. Her mother was very surprised.

"Where is the rice, Upik?" asked her mother.

"I am already tired of looking for it. I have even looked in the bushes. The rice has disappeared and left no trace. Perhaps someone has stolen it," answered Upik.

"It is impossible, Upik. Didn't I hide it neatly yesterday? It is really incredible that someone could have known about it," replied her mother.

"Mother, if you don't believe it, look for yourself. Let us go there together," said Upik. Soon they went to the swamp.

Arriving there, Upik's mother immediately looked into the bushes where she had hidden the remaining five *sukat*s of rice. It was not there.

She was surprised and didn't believe what had happened. Soon she looked into the other places, too, near the swamp. Suddenly she saw disturbed mud. Upik's mother was suspicious; perhaps there was something hidden in there. She tried to stir up the place around the mud. Under it there was the sack with the five *sukat*s of rice in it.

She lifted the sack. But what could she do? The rice in the sack was already mixed with mud. It was dirty and looked disgusting.

Upik's mother couldn't contain her anger. It must have been Upik who did it. She lost her patience. She regretted spoiling her daughter.

"Why did you do this, Upik? Don't you know that I work hard to provide for and raise you? You have gone too far!," said her mother, almost yelling.

"It was I who drowned the rice," replied Upik, "I do not want and am not able to bring it. Why did you force me in the first place?"

Her mother answered, "Upik, you are really an ungrateful child. How tirelessly I worked to look for a living, but you didn't appreciate it. You neglected the outcome of my work, after I made such effort and sweat for it. And you drowned it in the swamp just like that."

Her mother was so angry, she could not say another word. Upik heard her mother's last words, "I hope *you* do not drown in this swamp."

After saying that, Upik's mother went home. She carried the sack of the rice that now was dirty and mixed with mud. She kept on walking and left Upik. She never looked back.

Upik was dazed and alone. She followed her mother home. But after just a few steps, she slipped and fell into the swamp. Her body gradually sank.

Upik screamed for help to her mother, but her mother was too far away to hear. Upik kept on crying and asking for forgiveness of her mother. Nothing could be done. Her mother never looked back. She kept walking, thinking about her ungrateful child.

Eventually Upik sank to the bottom of the swamp (or *rawa* in the local language). Only her shawl was visible on the surface of the swamp.

Later people named the swamp Rawa Tekuluk (tekuluk means shawl). People say that the swamp remains a terrifying place to this day.

BATU BADAUNG

A folktale from Ulath Village on Saparua Island in South
Maluku Province

There once was a poor widow whose life was difficult. Her husband had been dead a long time and she tried to support her two children alone. Every day she would go out to try and find enough food for her little boy and girl to eat. Sometimes when the tide was low, she could find sea creatures to bring home for their meal. On the shore near their home stood a huge rock with a strange shape that looked like leaves. It was called Batu Badaung, Leafy Stone.

One day when the mother searched the beach for food, all she could find was a long fish. It was long and skinny like a snake. She brought it home and cooked it for her children. "Don't eat it all," she warned. "I may not be able to find food tomorrow. We must always save enough for at least one more day, in case of bad luck."

The next day she rose at dawn, hoping to find something better for their meal that day. But she had no luck at all and returned exhausted and hungry at day's end, thinking of the leftover fish head at least.

But when she got home she found that her children had eaten every scrap of the fish. There was nothing at all left, not even the head. She was sad that they hadn't saved something. They had not thought to keep even a bite for their mother.

The mother went to bed hungry and dragged herself out of bed next morning to try again to find food on the shore. But once more she failed to discover anything at all that she could bring back to her children. In despair, the exhausted mother approached the huge rock, Batu Badaung, and began to sing:

"Batu Badaung,
please open your mouth
and swallow me.
Since life is so difficult,
I don't know what to do.
I am so sad.
Please swallow me."

It was almost dark now, and the daughter had come to the shore to see why their mother did not return.

She saw her mother singing to the rock:

"Batu Badaung,
please open your mouth
and swallow me.

Since life is so difficult,
I don't know what to do.
I am so sad.

Please swallow me."

And a third time, the distraught mother sang this song:

"Batu Badaung,
please open your mouth
and swallow me.

Since life is so difficult,
I don't know what to do.
I am so sad.

Please swallow me."

Suddenly the stone opened!

The mother jumped right into the stone. And it closed again over her.

Only one arm was left dangling from the stone's huge side.

The little daughter ran up and began to tug on her mother's arm. But it was in vain. The stone had swallowed her mother.

Her mother would be seen no more. The girl cried:

"Batu Badaung
Spit out my mother!

Batu Badaung,
Throw her up!

Batu Badaung,
Spit out my mother!

Batu Badaung
Throw her up!"

Clutching her mother's arm and crying and crying, the little girl did not notice the rising tide. Suddenly she was swept off her feet and carried to the shore. She ran to the village sobbing. But there was nothing anyone could do to save her mother.

The tide continued to rise, higher and higher, until the entire stone was covered with water. In came the tide, until it flooded the shore to a depth never before seen.

And never did the tide recede again far enough to reveal the huge stone Batu Badaung. The stone and all within it had been reclaimed by the sea.

Stories About Rice

Rice is the staple food of most Indonesian people. Each culture has its own stories about rice. Since many kinds of rice are grown, each has its own story, such as rice that grows in the wet field and rice that grows in the dry field.

In the past stories about rice were usually told as part of a ritual ceremony or at the beginning of the planting season. This ceremony is seldom performed nowadays. Those whose staple food is other than rice also have their own stories about the foods they eat, such as stories about sago (Maluku Province) and corn (Madura Island).

In many stories gods and goddesses were associated with rice. They gave rice to humankind or taught people how to cultivate, harvest, and store it. See, for example, *The Origin of Rice in Java Island* and *How Rice Grows in the Wet Rice Field*. Self-sacrifice to purify the world (mostly done by women) is the main point of stories about rice in the stories here from Flores and Central Kalimantan Province.

WHY RICE GRAINS ARE SO SMALL

A folktale from West Kalimantan Province

A long time ago, people say, rice grains were not as small as they are nowadays. They were as big as a coconut! In those days, when people wanted to cook rice, they had to cut the huge grain into small pieces.

In a village lived a mother with her daughter. They lived modestly and thriftily even though they had a lot of rice stored in their rice barn. Since one rice grain was as big as a coconut, they just shelled the skin and cut the large grain into pieces when they cooked rice. And they didn't need to dry the rice first, as we do today.

One day when the mother was busy with her work, she told her daughter to cook the rice. "Daughter, I have to finish my work first. Cook rice for our meal. Measure out the rice. *Satu iris satu periuk, satu gantang satu belanga.* A slice for a small pot, a *gantang* for a large pot."

After listening to her mother's order, the girl took a small slice of rice and put it in a cooking pot. From that time on the girl was ordered to cook rice every day.

But every day the girl would forget how much rice to put in the pot. She always asked her mother, "Mother, how many kilos of rice do I have to measure?"

The mother always replied,

Satu iris satu periuk,
satu gantang satu belanga.

One slice for one small pot,
one *gantang* for one large pot.

Every day the daughter and mother had this conversation about how to cook rice.

One day the mother had to go to a river in the forest to look for fish. Before she left, she reminded the girl, "Daughter, don't forget. When you cook the rice, take only a small slice. And take good care of the house while I am gone." After saying this, the mother left.

In the evening, when it was about time to cook the rice, the girl went to the rice barn. She was confused by now, and she couldn't remember her mother's message. She just couldn't remember how much rice she should take from the rice barn.

She thought and thought. Then she began to talk to herself. "How many *gantang*, how many *gantang*."[*] She kept saying the words. She had forgotten that she had to cook only a small slice of rice as her mother had told her.

As her house was surrounded by forest, many animals lived nearby. Suddenly from behind the bushes a Kuai chameleon began to answer her. "*Dua gantang. Tiga gantang.* Two *gantang*. Three *gantang*."

The Kuai kept repeating his words. "Two *gantang*. Three *gantang*. Two *gantang*. Three *gantang*."

Listening to this answer, the girl, without thinking, took a grain of rice the size of a coconut. She put the whole huge grain in the pot and began to cook it on the fire.

After a while the rice began to boil. It boiled and boiled. But there was so much rice in the pot that it boiled over. Rice spilled from the pot and began to roll on the floor in every direction. More and more rice!

When the girl's mother came home there was rice EVERYWHERE!

All this spilled rice turned into small single rice grains. And since that day, rice grains have been as tiny as those spilled drops.

---

* The accurate measurement of one *gantang* is 6.875 pounds (3.125 kilograms).

THE ORIGIN OF RICE
ON JAVA ISLAND

A folktale from Central Java Province

A long, long time ago, on the island of Java there were no rice plants. The people of the earth had only cultivated cassava for their daily food. Rice was only permitted to be cultivated in heaven. At that time rice was the food of the gods.

At that time also the relationship between human beings and the gods was very close. Man was permitted to visit heaven by walking along the clouds. The gods and goddesses also often descended to Earth to chat with man.

One day a youth went to Heaven. He happened to see the gods dining on food that he hadn't seen on Earth. The youth didn't know that the food he saw was rice.

The fragrant smell of the rice made the youth's mouth water. How he wished to taste the delicious rice!

He sought a way to get his wish. He went to see Dewi Sri, the goddess of rice. He mustered up the courage to beg Dewi Sri to be permitted to stay in Heaven and to learn to cultivate rice.

He said, "Dewi Sri, Goddess of Rice. I beg to be permitted to stay temporarily in Heaven. Please allow me to help plant, harvest, and pound your rice. Even if I get only a handful of rice, I want to help. I want to taste this rice, even if only a little."

Dewi Sri, who was wise and kindhearted, agreed. "Did you know that rice comes from this plant?" She showed him a rice plant. "You may work here and learn to be a farmer and cultivate rice."

How joyful was the youth to get permission to stay in Heaven. Dewi Sri taught the youth how to plant rice. First she taught him how to plow the rice field with a kind of tool to turn over the soil. It was called a *waluku.*

Waluku.

Then she taught him how to soften the soil with a harrow called a *garu.*

Garu.

After the soil was softened, the youth learned how to irrigate, raise seedlings, plant, and harvest. When the rice plant ripened, the goddess showed him how to cut the stalk using a small palm-held reaping knife called an *ani-ani.*

Cutting rice using ani-ani.

Dewi Sri also taught the youth how to pound the rice in a rice mortar called a *lesung*.

When all of this work was done, the youth was at last allowed to taste a small handful of the rice. It was delicious! Just as he had imagined it would be.

The youth stayed on in heaven and learned rice farming well. He also enjoyed delicious rice many times.

But after several years of hard work as a farmer in Heaven, the youth decided to go back home to Earth. He longed for his family, relatives, and neighbors.

"How happy they would be if the people in Java Island could enjoy this delicious rice," he thought. "By eating rice, the people could become as healthy and strong as the gods."

The youth approached Dewi Sri and asked permission to descend to Earth to visit his family and friends, whom he had not seen in such a long time. Dewi Sri agreed. But very early in the morning, without the gods' knowledge, the youth took several ripe rice stalks. He carried them with him to Earth.

Arriving on Earth, the youth planted the rice grains in just the way he had learned in Heaven. The rice grew rapidly. He worked hard and his plants developed well.

A farmer plants rice.

As soon as he had a harvest, he gave rice seeds to all of his neighbors and showed them how to plant and care for the rice.

Eventually all places in Java Island were covered with rice plants. When the rice was ripening for harvest, a golden yellow color covered the entire land of Java Island.

One day the gods came to visit Earth. How startled they were to see golden rice plants stretching in all directions. They hurried back to heaven and reported to Dewi Sri. The gods were furious. Rice was permitted only in heaven.

Dewi Sri descended to Earth. She knew this must be because of the youth who had helped cultivate rice in Heaven. He must have stolen the rice seeds when he left Heaven.

She soon met that youth.

The Origin of Rice on Java Island 73

At first Dewi Sri was furious, "Young man, why did you betray my trust? You should not have stolen rice. This is the food of the gods."

"Forgive me, Dewi Sri," said the youth. "I took the liberty of bringing rice seeds back from Heaven without asking permission first. I did not do this for my own interest, Dewi Sri. I brought this rice back for the benefit of all the people in Java Island. These people had only cassavas to eat. I took pity on my fellow men and shared with them the rice seeds so that they also could taste delicious rice. I know I have angered you, Dewi Sri. I am willing to accept punishment for what I have done."

Dewi Sri's anger subsided. The kindhearted youth had intended to do something sincere and lofty because he thought of other people.

"I forgive you," replied Dewi Sri. "But you should always ask permission first and not take things by stealing. As punishment for this, I will never allow another human to come to Heaven, the place where the gods live.

"However," she continued, "You will be allowed to cultivate this rice. But take notice that this rice plant is like my child. Take good care of it just as I have taught you."

Dewi Sri gave explicit instructions. "Irrigate the rice field regularly. Weed the wild plants around the rice plants. Fertilize the soil. Harvest carefully with the *ani-ani* knife, so that you do not waste any grains or damage them. Let the birds also enjoy a bit of the delicious rice. Don't kill them, because the birds are the beloved animals of the gods. If you don't pay attention to my order, I will send disaster to destroy your work." That was Dewi Sri's advice.

Before Dewi Sri flew back to heaven, she spoke once more. "In order to make the rice plants grow best, follow nature's rules. Plant the rice at the right time. I will give a sign from heaven by dropping jasmine flowers from my hair bun. These flowers will become *waluku* stars (Orion). This is the sign that the season for planting has come."

Bintang waluku.

Even today Dewi Sri's ruling is followed. When the waluku *stars appear in the night sky, the following day the farmers will start to plant their rice.*

The rice plants will grow rapidly and fill the soil of Java Island if the farmers pay attention to Dewi Sri's message. If they neglect Dewi Sri's orders, she will send an infestation of mice to attack the rice plants.

To remind them of Dewi Sri's order, the people in Java Island hold various ceremonies to ask forgiveness and to avoid disasters. Meduni *is a ceremony to start planting rice with prayers and offerings. A small* keris *dagger is embedded in the dikes between rice fields to prevent disasters.*

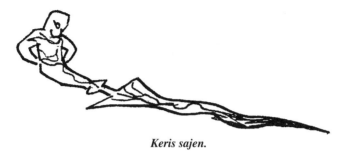

Keris sajen.

The ceremony wiwit *is held when the rice is ready to harvest. With prayers and a ritual meal, a wooden doll symbolizing Dewi Sri is put in the middle of the rice field as a token of gratitude to Dewi Sri.*

Boneka Dewi Sri.

Sesaji.

All the villagers work together to harvest the ripe rice. The workers who help harvest are paid with rice. Each is given one sewuli *for each* sekampil *of rice harvested.*[*]

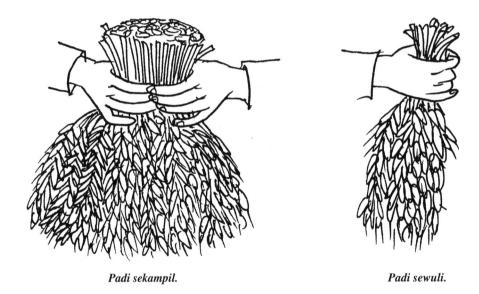

Padi sekampil.   *Padi sewuli.*

After the harvest work is done, the doll of Dewi Sri is put on the stack of rice in the rice barn to keep the rice free from attacks by mice.

After all the work is done, the ceremony of pounding rice in mortars is held. This work is done together in groups. As the rice is pounded a beautiful rhythm is created that echoes through the whole village as a sign of the happiness that is felt by all the people.

---

* *Sewuli* is a measurement made touching the thumb to the index finger on one hand only. *Sekampil* is done by touching the thumbs to the index finger of both hands

THE ORIGIN OF RICE

A folktale from Flores in West Nusa Tenggara Province

An old story recounts that there was once a man who appeared from the soil. This man was named Koke Tulit. He brought fire with him.

Already at that time on the earth there lived a woman called Nini Bunga Majo Mae. Everyday Nini ate raw food because there was no fire on the earth.

One day the two met. They married and became husband and wife. As Koke Tulit knew about his wife's circumstances, he taught her how to cook and they began to eat cooked food.

This husband and wife soon had a son named Pati Lae. When he became an adult, Pati Lae married a sea fairy named Gomi Bura.

Pati Lae and Gomi Bura had eight children, seven boys and one girl, called Nogo. The brothers' names were Laloku, Lalera, Latimu, Lawarat, Lalode, Bala, and Harut.

One day Nogo asked her seven brothers to work on the family farm.

After they had finished and the farms were ready to plant, the brothers asked Nogo, "Nogo, the farms are ready now, what are we going to plant?"

"You must plant me," answered Nogo. "You must kill me and plant *me*." Nogo's seven brothers all refused to do this thing. They didn't have the heart to kill their beloved sister. Even though she repeated this request many times, not one of her brothers would do this.

At last, after many days Bala summoned up the courage to fulfill his sister's wish. But before Nogo's request was carried out, she gave her message to Bala: "Take me into the middle of the farm. Mince the meat of my body and spread it all over the farms. But remember, don't leave me alone there in the fields."

Bala did as his sister ordered. And he did not leave the fields. He stayed beside them, as his sister had ordered.

On the eighth day Bala saw rice growing all over the farm. During that time Bala had never come home, because he had to look after his sister who was in the farm. Bala looked after the rice, which was the incarnation of Nogo, until it had born fruit and yielded a harvest.

When harvest time came, Bala went back to his village to call his other brothers. They harvested the rice together and built a rice barn to store their harvested crops.

After they had stored the crops in the rice barn, the seven brothers went home. Arriving home, their mother asked for their sister. She was not with them.

Nogo's brothers tried to think up answers to their mother's question. One said that Nogo was looking after a cockatoo on the farm. The others gave various reasons.

The mother said, "Listen, tomorrow all of you have to bring Nogo home."

But on the following day they still came home without Nogo. Their mother became very angry and decided to find her beloved daughter herself.

The next morning, Nogo's mother followed them to the farm. Arriving at the farm, she questioned Nogo's brothers, "Where is your sister?"

"Sister has gone home already," answered Nogo's brothers.

Their mother went directly home to see her daughter. But when she arrived there, her daughter was not at home. So she asked again, "Where is Nogo?"

"Nogo is over there," answered Nogo's brother. But their mother did not see Nogo. Only a heap of rice was piled up in the place where Nogo's brothers pointed.

Nogo's mother became furious. She took a knife and stabbed the heap of rice. That rice scattered all over the place. It rolled out the door and down the road.

Seeing what their mother had done, Nogo's brothers spoke to the rice. "Nogo, please don't run. Mother didn't mean to be angry at you. She was angry at us brothers."

But the rice had scattered everywhere.

Ever since then rice is found in all of the villages, because Nogo ran to other villages at that time.

People also say that rice is found in other places because Nogo's brothers didn't listen to her advice. She told them to cook only one grain of rice at a time, so that the rice would not spill out of the cooking pot. But in the beginning they put in a lot at once and the rice spilled everywhere. Because of this, Nogo became angry and talked to them in their dreams. "You didn't listen to my message, so I have run away to the other villages."

Note: According to the source of the story, this story is no longer performed and is now only told as a bedtime story for children.

THE ORIGIN OF RICE

A folktale from Central Kalimantan Province

There was once a village called Tanah Lingo. At one time a long dry season occurred in Tanah Lingo. No plants grew, the wood became dry, and wildfires started often. The rivers had no water and many of their stones were cracked because of the extreme heat of the sun's rays.

The danger of starvation threatened the villagers. The head of the village was worried about how to face this bad situation.

As there was no one who could solve this problem, the villages entrusted the situation to a *datu*. The *datu* was leader of all the village headmen.

Beritu Taun, the *datu*, undertook this heavy task. He meditated over possible causes of the bad situation that threatened his people. After much meditation, he found that many of the villagers had violated prohibitions of their ancestors. Many had also committed sins, done evil things, and shown hostility to others.

It was decided that to receive forgiveness from the ancestors, one of them must volunteer to sacrifice his soul.

Beritu Taun explained this to all of the villagers, but not one would sacrifice his soul to make up for the sins of the village.

Someone suggested that they hold a lottery to decide which person would give up his life. But this idea was rejected because the person had to give up his life voluntarily.

Some villagers did not even care about the bad situation that threatened. They felt the world should end in such destruction if that was destined to happen.

While the people argued about who should be sacrificed, Princess Liung appeared before her father, Beritu Taun. She said that she was prepared and willing to sacrifice her life to make up for the sins that had been committed.

All the family panicked at hearing the wish of Princess Liung. She was the most beloved daughter of her parents. Her relatives advised Beritu Taun not to accept his daughter's offer. They hoped somebody else would voluntarily step forward.

Beritu Taun's wife begged him to find someone else to be sacrificed. But as leader of the village it was difficult for him to refuse his daughter's sincere offering.

Again and again Princess Liung urged her parents to grant her wish and allow her to make a sacrifice for her people.

Eventually Beritu Taun announced to the people that his daughter had been chosen by the ancestors. Beritu Taun then hit a pole using a bamboo stick filled with small stones as a sign that a final decision had been made.

All the villagers were amazed and paid respect to their *datu*, Beritu Taun, the leader of the village heads. This leader held the customs and traditions so fervently that he was willing to sacrifice his own beloved daughter.

Two guards were assigned to execute Princess Liung. She was brought to the place of the sacrificial ceremony. Many people went with her.

In an open field where the ceremony was to take place, the whole village assembled in throngs, crowding around to witness the ceremony.

In the middle of the field, Princes Liung stood upright dressed in the sacrificial costumes. The two guards executed their task and in a few moments Princess Liung had ended her life in that place.

Princess Liung's blood flowed onto the dry land. The face of the princess was still beaming as her body fell on the ground as a token of sacrifice to the ancestors.

At the time of Princess Liung's demise, lightning and thunder rolled. Dark clouds covered the sky as if in grief to accompany Princess Liung's soul. A few moments later heavy rain poured onto the surface of the earth.

All night long the rain came down incessantly, falling from the sky. Apparently the ancestors had forgiven the sins of the village. They had accepted Princess Liung's sacrifice.

The next day nature brightened up again. The plants started to become green. The whole village was dizzily happy because there was no more danger of starvation. The waters of the river flowed again, the woods became green, and the birds once more flew about.

Princess Liung's mother went back to the field to see the place where her daughter had ended her life. There she found beautiful plants that looked like grass. But each grass was bearing a stalk of grain. This was the first rice plant.

Princess Liung was transformed into rice grains. From that time on she was worshipped as the goddess of agriculture. Ever since that time, people have had rice.

Kindergarten children dressed in traditional regional dress celebrate Kartini's birthday every April 21. Kartini was the leader and one of the pioneers of Indonesian Women's Emancipation. Photograph by Suandi Bunanta.

Children of the Mayang Sari Theatre perform "Dol Music" with traditional instruments from Bengkulu Province. Photograph by Syukri Ramzan.

Rubber band play, a traditional children's game in Krawang, West Java. Courtesy of *Kompas Daily*.

A group of doll puppets, *Wayang Golek,* from West Java, used in performing the Ramayana story. Photograph by Suandi Bunanta.

A puppet shadow performance in Central Java, with a repertoire taken from folktales. Courtesy of *Kompas Daily.*

Lemang, a kind of rice cake wrapped in young banana leaves and molded in a length of bamboo, like those in *The Legend of a Mountain (Talang Mountain)* (see pages 114–116). The cake is cut when served. Nowadays these traditional cakes are sometimes filled with banana or red sugar. Photograph by Yusrizal KW.

During the Muslim New Year, many people sell *ketupat,* made of steamed rice wrapped in coconut leaves. This traditional food is a main new year treat, served with many other dishes. Photograph by Murti Bunanta.

A rice field on Lombok Island in the West Nusa Tenggara Province. Photograph by Suandi Bunanta.

A woman sells Indonesian spices at Pasar Klender, a traditional market in Jakarta. Courtesy of *Kompas Daily*.

A tea picker at a plantation in West Java. Courtesy of *Kompas Daily*.

The famous freshwater Toba Lake in North Sumatera Province. This lake stretches 87 kilometers (54.4 miles) in length and approximately 27 kilometers (16.9 miles) in width. *The Legend of a Lake (Toba Lake)* (see pages 97–99) is passed on from generation to generation. Courtesy of *Kompas Daily*.

Jakarta's Thamrin Street, the heart of the business center. Courtesy of *Kompas Daily*.

Various crafts with many functions are made from bamboo, rattan, and pandanus leaves. Photograph by Suandi Bunanta.

A Dayak woman from the Kayak Mandalam ethnic group in West Kalimantan. Photograph by Julia Aloy.

A feast at a circumcision ceremony for young boys in Bandung in West Java Province. The children are riding *sisingaan*. *Sisingaan* means "like a lion." Photograph by Visi Anak Bangsa.

Cultural heritage is passed on from childhood. Girl weaver at Sade Village on Lombok Island in West Nusa Tenggara Province. Photograph by Visi Anak Bangsa.

Balinese people are born artists. Even in childhood they demonstrate their skills. Courtesy of *Kompas Daily*.

HOW RICE GROWS
IN THE WET RICE FIELD

A folktale from Central Sulawesi Province

A long, long time ago, rice grew only in the woods and on dry lands called *tegalan*. This is the story of how rice came to grow in wet rice fields, *sawah*.

There once lived seven sisters. Youngest's life was very miserable because all her elder sisters hated and rejected her.

Finally she decided to leave her home and wander. Even so, her life didn't change much. If she asked food of the villagers, she got only some rice hulls. After some time her clothing became ragged. She lived all alone in a tumbledown wooden hut.

One morning, without her noticing from where it came, some warm rice appeared in her hut. She was so hungry, she ate the warm rice ravenously.

The next day, the same thing happened. And the next. For seven days this continued.

On the following day, Youngest went for a walk. She saw seven rice stalks. Carefully she began to tend these seven rice stalks. She cared for them, fertilized them, and weeded around them. Every day she went to look at the seven rice plants.

The rice grew rapidly. Youngest said to herself, "My rice is ripening now. I need to stay beside the field to keep away the birds and pests. But how can I build myself a hut to watch the rice?"

In the morning when she went to check on her rice plants, there was a little hut already built for her.

She sat in the hut and guarded her rice plants from attacks by insects and birds.

When the rice was ripe, Youngest said, "I won't be able to harvest this rice by myself. What can I do?"

But the next day, the rice was already stored in the rice barn. And a new beautiful house for Youngest stood beside it!

Youngest was astonished at the miracles that had occurred.

A few days later, a man named Buriro came by. He was actually a god sent to live on Earth.

"Youngest, your life was miserable before, but I gave you food. You had no home, but I made one for you. When you had no rice, I prepared it for you. Now you should become my wife," said Buriro.

"I accept your proposal since you showed faith in me," said Youngest. "I know that you too must be miserable, since you are forced to live on Earth even though you are really a god."

So the two were married.

Ever since that time, rice that was planted in the forest would not grow. People were dying of hunger. Those who were still alive wandered until they came to the place where Buriro and Youngest lived. They were surprised to find a big, beautiful house overflowing with food.

Among these people were Youngest's sisters. They summoned up the courage to ask for work as servants for Youngest and to beg for food.

Youngest was so beautiful that the girls did not dare to look on the face of this princess-like person.

"Don't ask for food from me," said Youngest. "I am myself a poor person. I have no wealth at all."

Buriro heard this. "My wife, these are actually your own sisters who expelled and insulted you. Give them enough food."

The seven sisters then wept for each other. Youngest's sisters realized their mistakes and apologized to her over and over. Youngest felt happy to meet her sisters again.

Her sisters and the other people who came were permitted to live there and help work in the rice fields.

Many people followed in this work and eventually people realized that it would be good to plant rice in wet rice fields. This new invention was passed on from generation to generation up until now.

Buriro and Youngest returned to heaven. Their duty on Earth was now finished. They had taught people on Earth how to cultivate rice in the wet rice field, the *sawah*.

Stories of How Things Come to Be

Indonesian cultures are rich in stories of how things came to be. The following stories are examples. These range from the humorous *Why Shrimps Are Crooked* to the sad story *The Banyan Tree*. The stories have a great variety and explain the origin of plants, animals, places, and people.

THE ORIGIN OF THE NAME OF KUNDI VILLAGE

A folktale from Bangka-Belitung Province

Kundi Village is one of the eight villages belonging to the Bangka-Belitung Province, established in Indonesia in 2001.

There are three versions of the origin of its name. Two of them are presented here.

A group of ship passengers came from Java Island. In the middle of their journey a sudden storm attacked their ship. They anchored and stayed temporarily someplace on the coast of Bangka Island.

Among the passengers were a group of women. As was the Javanese women's custom at that time, they wore their hair in buns and held by hairpins. This type of hairpin was called a *konde* in the Javanese language.

When the weather brightened, the group set sail again. But one of the women's hairpins fell in that place. It was then found by a local villager.

The local people had never heard the name of the hairpin in the original Javanese language, and they were not sure what to call it. So they named it "*kundi*" instead of "*konde*." Ever since then, the place has been known as Kundi. This is how Kundi Village got its name.

Another version says that there was once a place near the seashore of Bangka Island where Chinese and local people lived together.

One day the Chinese decided to leave the place to build their own village. They said, "Nge hi kun, nga ki di," which means, "You are there, I am here."

People then abbreviated the words into "Kundi," and named that place "Kundi." Even though they live in separate villages, they live in harmony and always work together.

WHY GOAT EATS GRASS

A folktale in the Dawan language from East Nusa Tenggara

Once upon a time there lived a monkey named Bae Kean Belo and a goat named Bae Kean Bibi. They were good friends. *Bae Kean* is a friendship term in the Dawan language, which is used by people in Tautpah Village.

One day the friends were walking at the edge of a big river. There grew a cluster of banana trees with ripe fruit.

Bae Kean Bibi saw the banana trees. At first he tried to keep them secret from Bae Kean Belo. He wanted to eat the bananas himself, but since he didn't know how to pick them, he had to tell the monkey, Bae Kean Belo, about them.

They then came to an agreement. Bae Kean Belo had the task of climbing and picking. He would get the fruits and Bae Kean Bibi, the goat, would get the banana skins.

In a second, Bae Kean Belo was already on the banana tree. But then his bad intentions appeared. He kept eating the fruits voraciously without thinking of his best friend, Bae Kean Bibi, who was waiting for the banana skins. His saliva streamed down. Bae Kean Belo didn't care. He didn't throw the banana skins down.

Bae Kean Bibi was annoyed and left. Apparently Bae Kean Belo was not his best friend anymore. He then hid in a hole in a hollow log, restraining his hunger and anger, to observe the wiliness of his best friend.

Finally Bae Kean Belo took pity on the goat. He went down and brought a bunch of bananas for Bae Kean Bibi. But his friend was nowhere in sight. Bae Kean Belo whistled as a sign for Bae Kean Bibi. Until the sun set he could not find his friend.

Each time he saw another animal, he asked for Bae Kean Bibi. Bae Kean Belo regretted his deed, but he could not find his friend again.

Meanwhile Bae Kean Bibi, who was hiding in the hole in a hollow log, could not restrain his hunger. Eventually he had to fill his stomach with green leaves and grass.

The goat, Bae Kean Bibi, took an oath that his offspring would make grass and green leaves their main food.

WHY SHRIMPS ARE CROOKED

A folktale from Central Kalimantan Province

In Central Kalimantan people perform the tradition of mandep, *a kind of share work. If someone is doing large-scale work, such as building a house or harvesting rice, they will be doing* mandep *or receiving* mandep, *which more or less means to help.* Andep *refers to help received. If someone has ever helped someone else, in turn he or she will get help also when doing something.*

The following folktale tells about the tradition of mandep *through a story about a school of fish.*

There was once a school of fish who wanted to do large-scale work. Each of them planned to open a farm. Therefore, they decided that each in turn would help the others.

The idea first came from the *gabus* fish. Gabus's best friend, the *miau* fish, often came to visit. They were heard talking.

"My friend *miau* fish, what is your opinion about the forest fire that just happened?" asked the *gabus* fish of the *miau* fish.

"What do you think?" asked the *miau* fish in return.

"I think it would be good if we use the burned area for a huge farm, as we don't need to cut and chop down the trees," replied the *gabus* fish.

"Your idea really does make sense!" answered the *miau* fish.

"So won't it be better if we also invite other fish to have a meeting to discuss our plan? Then we can open a bigger farm," suggested the *gabus* fish.

"It is really a good idea. I agree with you. Let us invite the *saluang* fish, the *banta* fish, the *masaw* fish, and the others so that we can realize this work."

So the *gabus* and *miau* fish went to the house of each fish. They all were happy to hear the *gabus* fish's idea. All of them gladly responded and promised to come to the meeting the *gabus* fish was going to hold.

On a fixed day everyone gathered. There came also *balida, tabiring, manjuhan, patin, lawang, kakapar, bapuyu, sepat, lele, telan,* and many kind of scaly fishes and, not to be left out, the shrimp.

After all the invited fishes gathered, the *gabus* fish started the discussion. "Friends, today we gather to discuss a big work that needs to be shared. We are going to open a farm in the forest in the place where it has been burnt down. We need a chairman who will organize this work so that we can do it well."

All the fish agreed to what the *gabus* fish said. Among them there was the *masaw* fish. Masaw stood up and said, "I think the *tabiring* fish is the most appropriate to be the chairman."

Apparently the *lele* fish didn't agree and proposed another candidate: "Tabiring is strong, but we could also ask Tambahas to be the chairman."

Hurly-burly the fishes proposed candidate after candidate. But still they could not decide who was the most appropriate to be the chairman.

Finally the *saluang* fish was chosen. The *saluang* fish stood in the middle of the crowd and decided that the work had to start on the following day.

In the morning they left for the place where they wanted to work. Each set up a pole as a sign of the border of this farm.

The fish soon cleaned up the woods on their farms. Afterward they used sticks to make holes for planting the seeds. For making the holes they needed a lot of help, so they decided whose farm would be prepared for planting first.

So it was, on the first day the fish prepared the *manjuhan*'s farm. While the others were at work, the *manjuhan* fish prepared the food.

Soon Manjuhan started to cook because there were a lot of fish who were doing *mandep.* The *manjuhan*'s farm was large. After cooking rice, Manjuhan prepared the dishes, then considered for a while. Then Manjuhan took a big cooking pot and filled it with cold water.

What then? Manjuhan entered the pot. Not long after Manjuhan jumped out again from the pot. Apparently Manjuhan had laid eggs there.

Manjuhan then placed the pot that had been filled with eggs on a hearth, and afterward put a lot of vegetables in it.

At noon all the fishes went back to the hut to take a rest and have lunch. "*Manjuhan,* how delicious the smell of your food is! What kind of dish did you cook?" asked the fish.

"Look for yourselves and enjoy my cooking," replied Manjuhan. After a while the rice and the dish were done. All the fish ate together. The food Manjuhan prepared was delicious.

After they ate, the *kakapar* and *bapuyu* fish were talking about the delicacy of the *manjuhan*'s food. "*Bapuyu,* how clever is *Manjuhan.* Do you know how the food was prepared?" asked the *kakapar* fish.

Bapuyu was silent for a while, trying to think. "Well, Kakapar," said Bapayu, "before the dish was placed on the hearth, when the pot was just filled with water, Manjuhan entered into the pot and laid eggs there."

"What you said is right," answered Kakapar. "I also thought the same thing about how Manjuhan cooked. How really clever!"

After lunch the fishes went back to work until the day become almost dark. After finishing, before they went home, Manjuhan served the delicious food again.

After they had prepared Manjuhan's farm, the fishes moved to Balida's farm. It was the same there. Balida prepared food as delicious as the food Manjuhan had prepared.

Now it was the turn of the *tabiring* fish to get help. At Tabiring's place they also were served with food not less delicious than the food Manjuhan had prepared.

So it happened. They prepared each of the farms in turn, until eventually they came to the shrimp's.

Before they started to work, the *gabus* fish asked the shrimp, "Shrimp, what dishes will be for us today?"

"You do not need to worry. For sure it will be as delicious as the previous," answered the shrimp, smiling.

"Do you know how to cook?" asked Gabus.

"Everything will be fine; if they can do it, I surely can!" replied Shrimp confidently.

While the others were preparing the farm, Shrimp prepared the food. Shrimp built a fire in the hearth to cook rice.

"Well," Shrimp thought, "How do I cook the delicious meal like all my friends did?"

Shrimp thought for a while, then took a big cooking pot and filled it with water. Shrimp placed it on the fire. Not long after, the water started to boil. The smoke of the boiled water billowed. Suddenly, Shrimp jumped into the cooking pot.

Noon passed and Shrimp still had not called the friends to go back to the hut. All of them were waiting, but even when the sun had set in the west, there was no call from Shrimp.

"What has happened? Why is Shrimp so late? I am starving!" said the *masaw* fish.

"Yes, I am hungry, too," said the *banta* fish.

All the fishes grumbled. Until the day became dark there was no call from Shrimp. Finally, the *saluang* fish suggested that they stop for a while. "Friends, let us go back to the hut first and see what Shrimp is doing."

So the fish went back to the hut with nagging stomachs, restraining their hunger.

Arriving at the hut, the *saluang* fish called, "Shrimp, Shrimp, is the food ready?" But no one answered.

"What has happened to Shrimp?" asked the fishes of each other.

They looked in the hut. The fire in the hearth had already died out. The cooking pot was still on it. Even the rice that was done hadn't been taken out.

They all wondered, "Where is Shrimp?" They called, but Shrimp didn't answer.

After searching everywhere and not finding Shrimp, they started to eat. First they spooned out the rice, then each took the dish. Nothing strange happened.

But when the *patin* fish took the dish, suddenly Patin saw Shrimp among the vegetables. Shrimp's body was crooked and reddish. Shrimp was dead. All the fish were in an uproar after learning that Shrimp was dead, leaving a crooked body among the vegetables.

Because of Shrimp's foolishness in not asking the other fish how to prepare the food, the shrimp was dead. His stupidity caused his death.

People say that, ever since that time, when a shrimp dies, its body will become crooked. This will not happen to the fishes, though.

THE ORIGIN OF THE BANYAN TREE

A folktale from Central Java Province

Once upon a time there was a brave king who reigned in one of the biggest kingdoms on the island of Java. He could defeat his enemies with swords and spears or only with a dagger. It was said that he could catch more than fifty arrows with his bare hands. The countries he had conquered were numerous.

The king had a queen and several concubines. The queen and king had a son named Jamojaya, and his most beautiful concubine, named Dewi Andana, bore him a son named Raden Samijaya. The beauty of Dewi Andana exceeded the beauty of the queen and all the other concubines. She was also the one most deeply loved by the king. He often gave her jewelry and other expensive gifts.

The prince, Jamojaya, was loved and honored by all his people for his handsomeness, bravery, and strength. Moreover, he was very kind to everyone. Unfortunately the concubine, Dewi Andana, hated Jamojaya. She was jealous because her son, Raden Samijaya, was not a prince. Dewi Andana was afraid that when the king died and Prince Jamojaya succeeded him, she and her son might be thrown out of the palace. She tried to find a way to get rid of Prince Jamojaya.

One day when the king was visiting Dewi Andana, she pretended to look sad. When the king asked why she was sad, Dewi Andana said, "Forgive me, Your Highness, I have received so many beautiful and expensive gifts from you, but I still have one unfulfilled wish." "Say what you want, Dewi Andana. Your wish shall be granted," replied the king. "I want my son, Raden Samijaya, to become your heir." She said these words in a forceful tone.

The king was very surprised at her wish and, despite his promise, refused to fulfill her desire. It was impossible for Raden Samijaya to replace his brother, Jamojaya, for Raden Samijaya was not a prince. But Dewi Andana would not be silenced. "Your Highness, if Prince Jamojaya rules, all your concubines will be expelled, and you won't see me again. To avoid this, please tell Prince Jamojaya that there is someone who is plotting to poison him. So Prince Jamojaya has to leave the palace soon."

Continuously nagged by Dewi Andana, the king finally gave in. He called Prince Jamojaya and told him of his decision that the prince should leave the palace immediately. Hearing the king's order, Prince Jamojaya begged him, "Father, let me stay in the palace. I am not afraid of being killed if that is to be my destiny." But the king stuck to his decision, and no one could change his mind.

Prince Jamojaya sought out his wife, Princess Kusumasari, and told her about the king's decision. "Dewi Kusumasari, my wife, I have been asked to leave the palace. Although I have told the king that I am not afraid of being killed and want to stay, the king has refused to allow me to do so. I have to depart very soon. Since I will have to travel a long distance, it would be better for you to stay in the palace." But Dewi Kusumasari determined to go with her husband.

While Prince Jamojaya was talking to Dewi Kusumasari, Dewi Andana crept into Prince Jamojaya's room. She was worried that the king would feel sad at Jamojaya's departure and change his mind. She slipped poison into Jamojaya's drinking water, which he kept in a *kendi* (a clay pot) near his bed. Then she hurried out of the room. That night Prince Jamojaya felt thirsty and drank the poisoned water.

When Prince Jamojaya awoke the following day, he felt tired and had a headache, but he didn't tell anyone about his condition. A few days later, Prince Jamojaya left the palace accompanied only by Dewi Kusumasari. No bodyguards attended them as they went. Every day on the journey Prince Jamojaya grew weaker. Although he felt sick, he gallantly kept on walking into the forest beside his wife. Finally the day came when he could no longer keep going and he died.

Dewi Kusumasari was very sad and cried. Kneeling beside Prince Jamojaya, she prayed for help from the gods in heaven. Hearing her lamentation and prayer, the god Kamajaya, the Protector of Marriage, was touched and descended from heaven. When she noticed, from where she sat mourning, the god Kamajaya standing near Prince Jamojaya's body, she begged him: "Forgive me, God Kamajaya, have mercy and bring Prince Jamojaya to life again!"

The god Kamajaya answered sadly, "I am sorry I cannot fulfill your wish, my child ! Prince Jamojaya has drunk strongly poisoned water. No gods will be able to cure him. To make him live forever on Earth, I will change him into a strong and beautiful tree that will grow in this very place."

At first Dewi Kusumasari didn't understand what the god Kamajaya had said. Then suddenly she saw Prince Jamojaya's body stand upright with outstretched arms. His body was covered by rough skin and from his arms sprang green leaves. His long black hair became tangled roots that touched the ground. His legs disappeared into the earth, becoming underground roots. Dewi Kusumasari was not comforted by this strange tree. "What is this lifeless tree for? It is not my husband."

Then the god Kamajaya said, "Dewi Kusumasari, my child, remember that this tree is not lifeless. This tree is a sacred tree. It will be called *beringin* (the banyan tree) and it will live forever. All people will consider this tree sacred and put offerings for the gods under its branches. Kings who are weary of fighting wars will rest under the banyan tree while listening to the rustling of its leaves. Children will play in it, and youths will talk with their friends in its shade. But if any should dare cut down this tree, his descendants shall be cursed. They will sicken or suffer accidents before they grow up." Then the god Kamajaya flew back to heaven, leaving Dewi Kusumasari still mourning.

In her sorrow, Dewi Kusumasari approached the banyan tree, which was the incarnation of her husband, and hugged its trunk. Then she laid her head against its big trunk and went to sleep forever. Her soul was welcomed into heaven while her body turned into a spring of very clear water.

Meanwhile, in the kingdom riots were breaking out. All the people were anxious about the loss of the prince whom they loved so much. When the king announced that Raden Samijaya would succeed to the throne when he died, the people learned that Prince Jamojaya had been forced into exile. They grew so angry that riots could not be avoided, as they wanted Prince Jamojaya back in the palace.

Raden Samijaya, too, begged the king to allow Prince Jamojaya to return to the palace. He refused to replace his brother as prince. He not only loved his brother very much, he himself was only ten years old. One day Raden Samijaya disappeared from the palace. He had decided to look for Prince Jamojaya alone. The king ordered all his men to seek for Raden Samijaya. Although they searched all over the forest, no one discovered him.

After searching for some time, Raden Samijaya was unable to find Prince Jamojaya. He missed his brother very much. He prayed to the Supreme God to change his body into that of a bird. He thought that if he became a bird, it would be very easy for him to fly everywhere over the forests, mountains, rivers, seas, caves, and valleys to find his beloved brother. The gods heard Raden Samijaya's prayer. He was turned into a beautiful bird.

After changing into a bird, Raden Samijaya flew from forest to forest, mountain to mountain, and river to river, seeking Prince Jamojaya. One day he arrived at the place where Prince Jamojaya and Dewi Kusumasari had died. After drinking from the spring, he perched on a branch of the banyan tree. Sorrowfully, he called repeatedly, "Brother, brother, brother, brother. . . ."

No sooner had he finished calling than the leaves of the banyan tree could be heard in answer: "I am your brother. I am your brother. I am your brother." This was followed by a gentle cry from the spring: "You are sitting on your brother's lap. You are sitting on your brother's lap." Sadly the bird could not understand these words. He kept flying, seeking everywhere for his brother, calling: "Brother, brother, brother, brother. . . ." Although the banyan tree could be heard to answer: "I am your brother. I am your brother. I am your brother," the bird could not understand. And for all we know, he is still mournfully flying about to this day, seeking the brother he lost.

THE ORIGIN OF THE TRUNYAN PEOPLE

A folktale from Bali Province

As the story goes, on the north coast of Batur Lake in Bali grew a tree that soared high. Its leaves were thick and had many branches so that the tree became dense and comfortable for those taking shelter under it. The birds liked to sleep in the tree. The insects were attracted to the fragrance of its beautiful flowers. And the *tamulilingan* bees, who were black with yellow wings, liked to suck their pollen. Because the tree was so fragrant, the gods named it *taru menyan*.

Every day a beautiful goddess sat all day under the *taru menyan* tree. She sat on a heap of stones that surrounded the tree while watching the blueish water of the lake.

The pretty goddess also liked to sing. She was the most beautiful goddess, as if she had descended from heaven.

Suddenly the wind blew from the west, shaking the *taru menyan* tree and causing the fragrance of the tree to spread all around. The water of the lake rippled as if painted by the wind. What had happened?

After a while, three gods from heaven were seen flying above the lake and diving down to descend onto the *taru menyan* tree. They hung their wings on its branches and soon they plunged into the lake.

The beautiful goddess was startled. When they saw the goddess, the three gods paid homage and one of them, who seemed to be the leader, said, "Our deepest respect for you, Goddess! Hopefully all the gods protect us. The three of us came from Java Island and intend to look for the source of the fragrance that spreads all over the place. It seems that the fragrance comes from you and not from the water of the lake. Who are you?"

"I am the goddess who guards this *taru menyan* tree. The fragrance does not come from my body but from this tree," answered the beautiful goddess.

"We really want to have the fragrance. If you are magnanimous, please permit us to pick the flowers," asked the leader god again.

"Take as many as you like. Take good care of the seed of the tree and spread this plant," said the goddess again.

Apparently the god was not only attracted to the flowers of the *taru menyan* tree, he was also attracted to the beautiful goddess who guarded the tree.

"O, ye Goddess," said the god, "If the gods in heaven grant my wish, I would like to marry you."

"What did you say?" replied the goddess angrily. "Take your wings and leave this tree immediately. Go back to Java!"

But the god did not leave. Instead he came even closer and while he clenched his fist to his chest he said, "Before I own the *taru menyan* flowers and the guardian goddess, I won't go back to Java."

Soon he tried to catch the goddess's hand. But the goddess avoided him. She then quickly ran away. The god didn't give up. He kept chasing the goddess. Eventually after a long chase, the god caught the beautiful goddess.

As she could not get away, the goddess said, "The tradition of the gods' marriage indicates that a marriage will be considered legal if the god agrees to fulfill the conditions that the goddess sets forth."

"What are the conditions?"

"I am willing to marry you if you promise that after the marriage you won't go back to Java but will live in this region. Besides that, you will become the higher god of my people and the pole of this cosmos to prepare and take care of the welfare and life of our offspring to come."

Because of his great love, the god promised to fulfill all the conditions the goddess proposed. They then married and lived on the north coast of the lake.

Supposedly from the name taru menyan *came the name Trunyan. This is the name of a village located on the north coast of Batur Lake.*

The Trunyan people believe that they are descended from that god and goddess. The god is named Betara Gede Pancering Jagat and the goddess is named Ratu Ayu Pingit Dalem Dasar.

The two other gods who accompanied the journey of Betara Gede Pancering Jagat lived in the villages of Abang Dukuh and Kedisan. These two villages are also located on Batur Lake.

When people come to Trunyan Village, they can see a statue thirteen feet, two inches (4 meters) high made from stone that was kept in a meru.[*]

The statue is the materialization of Betara Gede Pancering Jagat. This god holds an important position in the traditions and customs of the Trunyan people to this day.

---

* A *meru* is a pagoda. It can consist of seven, nine, or eleven floors. The *Meru* in Trunyan is thirty-two feet, nine and a half inches (ten meters) in height and twenty-nine and a half inches (seventy centimeters) in width. It consists of seven floors. The statue in this *meru* is named Datonta

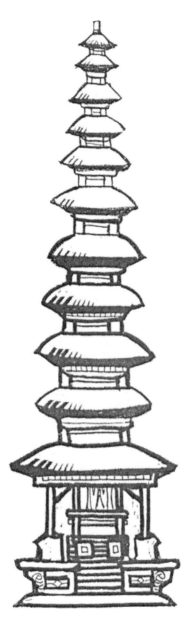

A *meru,* in Bali, like the one mentioned in this story.

Legends About Places

There are more legends about places related to the topography of the country than other types of legends. Each story is not merely entertaining but also contains a moral. Some show how people's relationships should be, such as husband and wife (*The Legend of a Lake*), wife and mother-in-law (*The Legend of a City*), and friends (*The Legend of a River*). Others deal with the environment.

THE LEGEND OF A LAKE (TOBA LAKE)

A folktale from North Sumatera Province

There was once a handsome youth who lived all alone in the world. His parents had left him a small farm. As he was very diligent, his life lacked nothing, even though it was simple. Sometimes he went fishing at the river. If he got enough fish, he would sell some to add to his earnings.

One day he didn't go to his farm. He felt like just going to the river to fish. Arriving at the river he set the net and waited patiently. Although he waited and waited, he caught not a single fish. He became annoyed and decided to go home that day without bringing any catch at all.

Suddenly his net was shaking. He tried to see what had been caught in it. Slowly he pulled in the net. It felt heavy. To the utmost of his strength he kept trying to lift his net.

"What has been caught there? Is it possible to get a big fish in this river? It is rather impossible," he thought while he kept pulling.

A few moments later, what did he see? A big fish with beautiful shiny scales, like diamonds struck by light, trying to get out of the net! She kept struggling to get herself loose.

The youth didn't want to release his fortune. He had waited the whole day, and this was his reward. The fish could be his meals for several days. Part of it could be sold. He kept hauling and dragging the net toward his home.

Arriving at home, the youth went directly to his neighbor's house. He wanted to borrow a bigger cooking pot to make curry of his catch. He left the big fish in his yard. As the houses in his village were located some distance from his, it took him some time to get back.

He was startled when he saw a beautiful girl cleaning up his house. Where did the girl come from? Why was she in his house?

"Who are you? Why are you in my house?" asked the handsome young man.

"I am the fish you just caught," replied the beautiful girl modestly, "I am destined to be the wife of the person who catches me."

The handsome youth was surprised. He didn't believe what he saw and heard.

The beautiful girl said to him, "I will live with you here and become your wife and take care of you. I also will help you. But there is one condition that you can't break. You have to keep the secret of my origin. Don't you ever call me 'fish' again. If you can give your word, I will live with you forever here."

Although the handsome youth felt as if he was in a dream, he was very glad and happy to have a beautiful wife who was adept at work. He promised to keep the secret of his wife's origin and loved her with all his heart.

So it was that the two became husband and wife. The neighbors wondered where his beautiful wife had come from. They were amazed by her beauty.

All this time people had known the young man as a quiet person who didn't have many friends although he was kindhearted. The handsome youth kept his wife's secret. He just smiled when he was asked about his wife.

Years passed by. The couple was blessed with a boy. He grew healthy and strong. The youth loved his wife even more and respected her. They lived happily.

But their son had a flaw. He liked to eat very much. Sometimes he didn't think about his parents. He just wasn't satisfied.

One day his mother asked him to take food to his father, who was working at his farm.

The son stopped on the way. His stomach felt empty. The delicious smell of his mother's cooking made his mouth water.

At first he tried to restrain himself, but then he couldn't do it. He opened the provisions he had brought for his father and ate them ravenously. He left only a bit. After enjoying his father's provisions, the boy hurriedly continued his way to the farm.

In the meantime his father was waiting. The day was extremely hot. He felt thirsty and hungry because he had worked since very early in the morning. He intended to take a rest and eat his lunch, but the food he waited for so long hadn't yet arrived.

When his son came bringing the remainder of the provisions that his wife had sent him, he became furious. It was bad enough that his food had become cold, but he also just got the leftovers.

"Where have you been? How naughty you are and insolent. I have been waiting for long. I have worked the whole day, but what I get is only the leftovers. Don't you know enough to leave something for others?" said the father furiously. He decided to go home.

His wife saw her husband coming with a gloomy and infuriated face. Her son was weeping. She heard her husband say, "Just like a fish's child, eating is the only skill!"

His wife was sad and disappointed at her husband's words. He had broken his own promise and moreover had humiliated her.

"My husband, you broke your promise. It is not right that you revealed my secret. I will go back to my origins. Take care of our child properly. I will leave this house soon," said his wife.

All of a sudden the earth began to shake strongly. A horrifying earthquake occurred. The water of the river where they lived overflowed and a terrifying flood rushed in, bringing disaster to everything in its path.

The villages sank and the houses fell into pieces carried away by the flood. The husband and son were dragged under the water and disappeared.

The water kept overflowing, and when it ceased a lake existed, which people called Toba Lake.

When a big fish is seen, that is a sign that the poor fish longs for her husband and son. She will appear if there are no people around the lake.

THE LEGEND OF A
HILL (BUKIT KELAM)

A folktale from West Kalimantan Province

A long, long time ago, a man named Bujang Beji lived in a village called Silat, which was located in Kapuas Hulu region. A river named Kapuas passed through this place.

This river had many forks, which formed the main waterway to reach this village, located far in the backcountry.

At that time there were a lot of kingdoms surrounding Bujang Beji's place.

That was why Bujang Beji thought, "I have to find a way that those people won't expand their territories and come to Silat through Kapuas River." Bujang Beji had determined to close up the channel of the Kapuas River.

Not far from Silat village there was a very high stone hill. As Bujang Beji had a divine power, he cut off the top of that stone hill.

Bujang Beji carried the piece that had been cut off on his back with a piece of rope wound around his body. The remaining part of the stone hill was later called Bukit Tunggul.

Along a narrow trail in the forest, Bujang Beji took the stone to a place called Sintang, where the Kapuas River met another river named Melawi.

Bujang Beji intended to close up the channel of the Kapuas and Melawi Rivers with the slab of stone, so that the ships from outside could not sail up and reach the place where he lived.

But unfortunately for Bujang Beji, when he reached a swampy area near Sintang, suddenly his leg was hooked on a root. The slab of stone that he carried fell off his back.

Bujang Beji tried hard to lift up the slab of stone using a lever stick and pushing off on a stepping stone. Because the pressure of his leg on the stepping stone was so strong, it caused the stone to disappear into the swampy area.

Later the stepping stone that sunk was named as Bukit Serentak. *Bukit* means a hill and se*rentak* means sinking.

Bujang Beji didn't succeed in lifting up the slab of the stone. He failed to fulfill his plan to close up the Kapuas and Melawi Rivers.

The fear that people from other kingdoms would enter their village brought a dark picture to the people of Sintang. That is why the stone that fell from Bujang Beji's back was named Bukit Kelam or Dark Hill. This hill now looks grandiose from the city of Sintang.

The people of Sintang believe that when the top of Bukit Kelam is covered by the mist of a cloud, in a few moments the rain will come. People have to be prepared, especially those who want to go by boat on the Kapuas and Melawi Rivers.

Grandiose Bukit Kelam or Dark Hill in West Kalimantan Province as seen from the city of Sintang. Photograph by Aloysius Aloy.

THE LEGEND OF A SWAMP (RAWA BENING)

A folktale from Central Java Province

Near the city of Ambarawa in Central Java province is a lake called Rawa Bening. Bening means "clear." (Often the name is given as Rawa Bening.) This is the story of how the swamp came to exist.

A long, long time ago a hermit lived with a son who had an ugly face. As this son wished to change his appearance, he went to live as a hermit in a dense forest. He then changed his form into a snake and coiled around a big tree.

Many years passed but the snake still kept living as a hermit. After a long time it joined with the tree and looked like its roots.

One day the villagers on the edge of the forest planned to hold a ritual meal or *kenduri*. They went in a group to the forest to look for prey that could be slaughtered and offered to guests at the ceremony.

Even though they had been looking for a long time, not a single animal could be caught. They felt tired, so they took a rest under a big tree with dense leaves.

One of them wanted to cleave an areca nut to chew betel. He put the areca nut on the roots of the tree. When his knife hit the roots, he was astonished to see them secrete resin that looked like blood.

The villagers were in an uproar when they found out that what they thought to be resin was actually blood. When they looked carefully, the roots were seen to be scaly.

Now people learned that what they thought was a root actually was the body of a big snake who was living there as a hermit.

They eagerly killed the snake and took the meat to offer in the *kenduri*. The meat of the snake was cut into small pieces and shared with those who went hunting.

After all of them received their meat, they went home. The villagers cooked the meat, making *satay* (meat barbeque), and performed the *kenduri*.

The soul of the snake who was killed transformed into a little ugly boy with a frightening face. His body was full of scabies and his clothes were ragged. He was crippled and his stomach was puffed up.

When the people were celebrating the *kenduri*, the boy went to their village. Of everyone he met, he asked for a little food, but no one wanted to give him alms. No one was willing to speak to him.

With an empty stomach he left the village and came to a small hut on the edge of the village. An old woman lived in that hut.

"Old woman, I am starving, no one of those who are celebrating *kenduri* care for me and will give me a little food. Can I ask you for a little food just to fill up my stomach?" said the boy to the kindhearted old woman.

"Of course, Son, but I do not have *satay*. I only have a little leftover rice. I am poor, and I am old. The people who were having *kenduri* do not remember me," replied the old woman.

"It is okay, Old Woman, this is fine for me," answered the little boy happily and immediately ate the food the old woman gave him.

After taking a rest, the little boy said farewell to the old woman and said, "Old Woman, I will go back to the village to see the people who are celebrating *kenduri*. If you hear the sound of a flood, get in a rice mortar immediately and bring along a rice ladle."

The old woman was surprised, but she promised to follow his advice. Soon the little boy left the old woman.

Arriving at the village, the little boy approached the children, who were playing and cheerful. Seeing the ugly little boy, crippled, in ragged clothes, they stopped their game and mocked him.

At first the boy was quiet, but then he said, "You are very arrogant and selfish. Show me, if you dare. Try a power struggle with me. Pull the palm leaf rib I stick in the ground. Each of you has to give me a piece of *satay* if you are unable to pull up this palm leaf rib."

While saying that, he stuck a palm leaf rib in a field where the children were playing. All the children laughed at his words. They looked down on the little boy. He was so thin and looked sickly.

Not long afterward, one of the children came forward arrogantly. "Look at this," he said, pulling on the leaf rib. But not a single inch did the palm leaf rib shift.

The other children were antagonized. One by one they tried to pull out the rib. But none could do it. The longer they tried, the more *satay* the little boy could collect. The people came to see what the uproar was about.

Now everybody tried. Almost all of the villagers came to see and try to pull the palm leaf rib out of the soil. But even the adults were not able to pull it out.

The Legend of a Swamp (Rawa Bening)   **103**

Finally, after nobody could do it, the little boy said, "Look, no one of you succeeded in pulling this palm leaf rib out. You are too arrogant and selfish. None of you shows a kind heart to the poor people who have a miserable life. All of these *satay* will be mine and you shall endure the consequences. You are stingy people."

He pulled the palm leaf rib out of the soil. The people were surprised to see water spurt from the soil where the palm leaf rib was drawn out.

The people ran to save their lives. The water became higher, flooding the entire village. The people ran back and forth in panic, while the little boy quietly disappeared.

When the kindhearted old woman heard the water starting to flood the village, she got in the rice mortar and rowed it with the rice ladle. She was the only one who survived.

Eventually the village was inundated with water and became a swamp with clear water. Ever since that time the village has been known as Rawa Bening.

Supposedly the soil that stuck to the palm leaf rib was flung far away and became a mountain called Kendalisodo. Kendali *means dirt and* sodo *means palm leaf rib. So the name means the dirt of the palm leaf rib. This mountain is located several miles from the city of Ambarawa, a small city in Central Java.*

As for the palm leaf rib itself, people say it became a snake that guards Rawa Bening. The old woman's rice mortar changed into a stone named Mengkelang, located in the Tuntang River, while the oar drifted away to a place that later was named Welahan. Welah *means "oar."*

People say the satay *became* keong gondang, *a kind of big snail.*

THE LEGEND OF A STONE (BATU PELANDUK)

A folktale from East Kalimantan Province

Batu Pelanduk is one of the names of the stones scattered along the upper course of the Mahakam River. The people of Dayak Bahau have stories about these stones.

Once a upon a time, people say, the top of Bato' Mili Mountain in East Kalimantan was very high, almost reaching the sky.

According to the story, at that time the people who lived surrounding that stone mountain were always in fear, because almost every night someone pounced on their cattle. The stables of the cattle were also in disorder.

Eventually the people agreed to watch surreptitiously and find out what kind of creature had disturbed the peace and quiet of their neighborhood.

After some time they discovered that the creature who disturbed them was a strange animal that descended from heaven to the earth through the top of Bato' (stone) Mili Mountain.

The people held a meeting. They agreed that they were going to share work to chop and cut down Bato' Mili Mountain so that the strange animal from heaven could not descend again to the earth.

At that time there lived a giant called Bengkaal. Bengkaal was the guardian of Mahakam River, and he lived there. Bengkaal's body was big and heavy. When he walked along the river his two hands pressed down the trees and plants that grew along the side of the river. That is why the trees and their branches along the Mahakam River always stoop in the direction of the river. This is because Bengkaal always walked back and forth in the river.

Even though Bengkaal's body was incredibly huge and his face was terrifying, he was not a mean creature. Bengkaal had a lofty heart and liked to help people. As the guardian of the Mahakam River, Bengkaal took care of the river diligently so that it would be clean and well maintained.

Since the people were so angry at the strange animal, they cut down Bato' Mili Mountain. Pieces of the stone flew into the Mahakam River, making the surface of the river full of big and sharp stones. Steep rapids developed.

The tumultuous noise startled Bengkaal, and he went looking for the cause. When he looked toward Bato' Mili Mountain; suddenly a piece of stone flew and pricked one of his eyes.

Bengkaal fell into the water, and with all the strength he had, he grasped the side of the river. People found Bengkaal spread out in the river and agreed to help him. Finally they succeeded in prying out the piece of stone that had entered Bengkaal's eye.

Through the medicinal treatment of the people of Dayak Bahau, Bengkaal was cured and continued to perform his duty cleaning up the stones that were scattered along the river.

Bengkaal kicked the stones, which were as big as a house, with his big and sturdy leg. He lined them up neatly. He carried out his duty diligently.

But the tumultuous noise caused by his steps, and the noise of the stones that he flung, disturbed some of the animals.

Pelanduk, the mousedeer, was annoyed by the noise. He looked for a way to stop Bengkaal. He gathered all the animals who lived in the forest and held a meeting. Everyone agreed to send the mousedeer to be their representative to see Bengkaal.

Bengkaal was sitting relaxed while fishing from a big stone. The mouse deer approached him. His clever but cunning brain kept looking for a plan.

The mousedeer said, "Bengkaal, your work troubles all the animals in the forest. We are disturbed because of your voice and your tumultuous behavior. And the children are frightened every day."

Bengkaal replied, "Mousedeer, I am a guardian of this river. It is my duty to take care of this river. It must be kept clean and taken care of, not befouled by the stone mountain. Who will do it except me? You can see for yourself how big the stones are. What can I do, I have to make noises."

The mousedeer said again, "I understand, but you disturb the peace of the inhabitants of the forest. Leave the stones scattered. You just take a rest, no need to make every effort."

"It is impossible, Mousedeer, it is my duty as a river guardian. I won't stop my work until it is done. Believe me, later my work will be useful to the human beings."

Seeing that Bengkaal stuck to his opinion and would continue to tidy up the scattered stones from the river, the mousedeer thought harder. He would be ashamed if he were not able to stop Bengkaal. What would the other inhabitants say? Wasn't he known as a clever animal?

Eventually the mousedeer thought of a trick, "Bengkaal! See what will happen? I will report you to the king of the jungle if you won't stop your work. He is very divine. If he gets furious, you will surely be killed. It serves you right, the result of your arrogance."

Although Bengkaal was threatened by the mousedeer, he was not afraid. He said, "Be my guest, I will wait for him."

The following day Bengkaal waited patiently. He intended to explain to the king of the jungle the benefits of his work.

Early in the morning the mousedeer asked his friends to climb up the hill. From the hill they then rolled big stones into the river where Bengkaal was waiting.

When the stones were rolling, the voice of the mousedeer called, "Bengkaal, my king is furious. He feels insulted. It is inconceivable that you who are only a stupid river guard dare to meet my king who is very divine."

All at once, on the mousedeer's command, a big stone was rolled at Bengkaal. The big stone glided over speedily, almost hitting Bengkaal.

Although Bengkaal had a huge body and strong muscles, he was not an arrogant creature who liked to make trouble. Bengkaal had a noble character and preferred to give in. He thought that it was no use to fight with the jungle king because it would bring even more disorder to the river and forest.

Seeing and hearing the madness of the king of the jungle, eventually Bengkaal stopped his work. Ever since that time, he has never put the scattered stones in order. He did not know that it was only the mousedeer's cunning trick.

This is the stone people believe pricked one of Bengkaal's eyes. There are folk stories about many stones scattered around and along the upper course of the Mahakam River. Photograph by Flora A. Moerdani.

This story explains why the upper course of the Mahakam River is full of large stones, causing the water of the Mahakam River to be full of rapids and vicious.

Not infrequently, people who embark on the Mahakam River become its victims. Many boats founder and break up when they collide with the rocks as big as houses that are heaped up here and there in the river.

To avoid accidents, every passenger on a boat gets off and walks on the side of the river, which is full of stones. Among others are the stone of Bengkaal's hat, or "Topi si Bengkaal" in the local language.

According to the story, after Bengkaal stopped his work, he felt disappointed. He went back to his place and threw up his hat, which had a pointed shape. Supposedly his hat later became a stone that had the shape of a pointed hat.

Beside the stone that originated from Bengkaal's hat, there is another stone that is believed to be the stone that pricked one of Bengkaal's eyes.

The big stone where Bengkaal sat while he was fishing is believed to be located in a place belonging to Mamahak Teboq Village. People say that this big stone has a hollow caused by Bengkaal, who sat on it.

The stone that was rolled by the mousedeer and his friends when they attacked Bengkaal is named Batu Pelanduk or the Mousedeer Stone.

THE LEGEND OF A CITY (BANYUWANGI)

A folktale from East Java Province

Banyuwangi is a city on the east coast of East Java Province. Banyu *means water and* wangi *means fragrant. From this town people can cross to Bali Island by ferry or boat. And this is the story.*

A long time ago ruled a king with the help of a chief minister who was handsome and dashing. He was also trusted by the king.

The chief minister had a beautiful wife, but as she didn't come from a noble family, his mother didn't like her. Therefore she was always trying to get rid of her daughter-in-law.

On one occasion the chief minister's mother found a way. She went to the palace to see the king. There she persuaded him to send her son to a faraway place so that he could not come back quickly.

The king then commanded his chief minister to go to the top of Ijen Mountain to pick a flower that has a special power: Whoever put it on would forever be young and beautiful.

This flower would be presented to the queen. The king was sure that the chief minister couldn't get back quickly because he had to endure a difficult journey full with dangers.

Heavyhearted, the minister left his beloved wife, who was in the early stage of pregnancy. The chief minister obediently carried out the king's command. He said farewell to his wife and asked his mother to take care of his wife during his trip. The chief minister didn't realize his mother's bad intentions.

After some time, the chief minister's wife gave birth. One day, without her daughter-in-law's knowledge, the chief minister's mother took the baby and threw it into a dirty, smelly river.

The chief minister's wife was sad and miserable at losing her child. She suffered because she couldn't find her child, even though she had already looked in the forest and along the river.

The Legend of a City (Banyuwangi)   **109**

In the meantime her mother-in-law scolded and accused her of killing her own child. Finally the chief minister's wife became sick. Her body became very thin and weak.

Some years later, after enduring difficulties and dangers, the chief minister succeeded in bringing home the divine flower the king had asked for. He brought the flower to the palace.

After appearing before the king, the chief minister went home. He wanted to see his wife and child whom he had left for a long time. He longed for his family.

The chief minister's mother heard about her son's coming. Quickly she met her son and told him that his wife was a cruel mother. She had thrown her child into a dirty and smelly river flowing near her house. After that, she said, his wife pretended to be ill to cover her cruelty.

The chief minister became furious listening to his mother's story. He didn't realize his mother's hatred of his wife. He looked for his wife, who was lying quietly. When he saw his wife, he immediately drew his dagger.

Seeing her husband's intention to kill her, the chief minister's wife said, "My husband, what is my fault that you want to kill me? For what reason would you make your hand and dagger become dirty with blood? I am not guilty. If you want a proof that I am not the one that killed your child, please bring me to the river."

"Don't pay attention to your wife's words," said the chief minister's mother. "Kill your wife right away. She is just pretending not to be guilty." The chief minister's mother was afraid that her lie would be uncovered.

The chief minister took pity on his wife because of her condition. He led her by the hand to the river. When they came to the side of the river, the chief minister said, "My wife, as you said, prove yourself, if you are really not guilty."

"My husband, I will soon leave you. My life was really miserable all this time. I am not guilty. This river will become my witness. Later, if a fragrance lifts from this river, it will be proof of the truth of my words."

After saying that, the chief minister's wife jumped into the river. A few moments later a fragrance arose from the dirty black river. The water then became clear.

"Banyu wangi, Banyu wangi, The water is fragrant, The water is fragrant," cried the chief minister. "My wife is not guilty."

The chief minister regretted that he had followed his anger and hadn't listened to his wife. He should have investigated his mother's claim first.

Suddenly from the bottom of the river appeared two buds of beautiful flower. The big one was created from his wife and the small one from his child.

He heard a soft voice coming from the small flower. "Father, please notice, my mother is not guilty. It was grandmother who threw me into this river. My mother is not guilty."

Then the big flower bowed as if hugging the small one, and in a moment the two disappeared to the bottom of the river.

Since that time, a lot of people have lived near the clear and fragrant river. Finally that place became a city named Banyuwangi.

THE LEGEND OF A RIVER (SEMBRA RIVER)

A folktale in the Tehit language from Papua Province

There were once three friends, Serefle, Qalqomik, and Ogitwqarefe. They lived in a region called Qoi in East Irian Jaya (Papua). Their living was sufficient because the soil where they lived was fertile and they could easily find prey.

But although they were friends, there was something that annoyed Serefle. Ogitwqarefe was not fair in dividing their livelihood, such as sago, fish, and pork. Ogitwqarefe gave Qalqomik more than he gave to Serefle.

"Ogitwqarefe is really coldhearted in treating me, his own best friend, like this," complained Serefle deep down in his heart. His resentment and anger, which were restrained in his heart, always bothered his thoughts.

As he could not restrain his resentment and anger, Serefle left his birthplace, Qoi, and went to another place named Sriya. He took his wife and son, who was still small.

Serefle and his family then lived in Sriya and he didn't want to see his two friends, Qalqomit and Ogitwqarefe, again.

In the new place, Serefle cut down the woods, cleared the land, and farmed. His resentment against Ogitwqarefe didn't disappear. At that time his wife was pregnant with his second child.

One day Serefle went to the forest. He found a dead breadfruit tree. The root and branches of the dead tree had been eaten by the worms. The woodworms, which were plentiful, could be used as food. Serefle marked the tree before going home.

The following day Serefle went back to the place where he had found the woodworms. He brought an ax, which he put on his shoulder, and a *koba-koba,* which he tucked under his left armpit, to keep the worms. He took also his son, whom he carried on his back.

Serefle intended to pick the woodworms from the dried tree he had found the day before. Arriving there, he put down his son and put the ax and *koba-koba* on the ground.

After that Serefle cut the *awo* leaves, the leaves of a kind of rattan. Then he spread out the leaves on the ground near the breadfruit tree. Afterward he chopped down the tree and picked out the worms in it.

Meanwhile Serefle's son saw what his father was doing. He imitated his father. He plucked *renat* leaves that were growing there, and he spread them out above a pig's mud puddle near the breadfruit tree.

He then divided the worms on the *renat* leaves that were already spread out, while saying, "This is for me, that one for father, another one for mother, and also the other for . . . the pig in the stable. And . . . brother who is still in mother's womb gets one as well."

He had just finished his words, when suddenly a kangaroo passed carrying a hooked knife. Meanwhile a white turtle appeared from the ground. The earth shook and an earthquake occurred. The sound of thunder was heard and lightning bolts were seen repeatedly that afternoon. The soil cracked and trees toppled.

Serefle hurriedly moved away from that place. He put his son on his back, hung his ax on his shoulder, and tucked his *koba-koba* under his armpit. He then ran to the utmost of his strength.

Not long after, water began to spurt up. It came out from the ground that had cracked. The water then ran into a stream, following Serefle.

Wherever Serefle ran, the water kept following him. He remembered his wife, who was at home, and his pigs in the stable. Serefle ran to his house to tell his wife to flee to save her life. But Serefle could not free himself from the pursuing flood waters.

Finally his wife, his home, and his pigs were pounded by the flood, which kept chasing Serefle wherever he went. The faster he ran, the faster the water streamed after him, until Serefle came to the seashore.

Serefle could not run farther because his legs slipped into the *gelodok* fish's hole. He could not escape now, and with great fear Serefle screamed, asking for help, "Oh, help me, oh fish, oh rattan, oh nipa palm tree. Help. . . . Stone, stone, help us."

Suddenly Serefle, his son, and his ax were swallowed by the water and became stone. The flood kept flowing swiftly and washed away all things in its path. All humans and cattle that were covered by the water became stones.

Ogitwqarefe, Serefle's friend, who lived at the seashore, was also swept away. Some capes of land were broken off, and these became islands.

The stone that is believed to have originated from Serefle still exists and is named nawqro, *which means a man who stands upright. The stream of the flood later became a river called Sembra.*

This is the story of the Sembra River, which exists because Serefle and his son picked woodworms and put them in a mud puddle.

Parents from the Tehit Society advise their children not to resent other people as Serefle resented his friend Ogitwqarefe.

If you go to the estuary of the Sembra River, there are a lot of fish and also a lot of mangrove and nipa trees. According to the local people, the trees originated from Serefle's cries for help.

The Sembra River's water is blue or green. That is why this river is also named blue river or green river.

If one stands beside the Sembra River near the nawqro *stone and says, "Nawqro, I have heard a lot of your beauty. Please, show me your fishes," thousands of fish of every kind will appear on the surface of the water.*

People who say these words have to have good intentions and cannot be planning to kill or catch the fish.

Note: *Renat* leaves are believed to be tabu for wrapping food, particularly sago worms and pork. The hooked knife mentioned in the story is fastened to a long bamboo stick and used to cut things that are too far away to reach. According to belief, this kind of knife was used by an underground creature to cause flooding and other natural disasters. Today the region of Qoi, from which this story comes, sticks out far into the sea and forms a stone cape. Nearby there are many small islands. In the Tehit language people do not distinguish between the colors blue and green, so the Sembra River is named both blue river and green river.

The Legend of a River (Sembra River)

THE LEGEND OF A MOUNTAIN (TALANG MOUNTAIN)

A folktale from West Sumatera Province

Once upon a time there lived a beautiful girl. The villagers named her Upik Manih. This girl was kindhearted, diligent, and adept.

Upik Manih's father was long dead, so she lived with her old mother, Mande. As she was the only child, her mother loved her very much. They both earned their living selling *lemang*, a kind of rice cake molded in a bamboo shoot.

Every two days, at night, they cooked *lemang*. And very early in the morning they went to the market to sell them. It was what they did every day to make their living. Upik Manih helped her mother industriously and never complained.

One day after coming home from selling, they went to cut down a bamboo to make *lemang*. The bamboo trees grew near their hut. As usual, they first chose the right bamboo to use as a *lemang* mold.

Just when they were about to cut down a bamboo, they heard strange noises coming from the biggest one. As time passed the noises became louder and louder until finally they sounded like human voices.

Hearing this, Upik Manih and her mother decided not to cut down the bamboo tree. They were very frightened. They had never heard such noises.

The sounds kept coming from the direction of the bamboo tree. They became even more terrified. Just as they were about to run and leave the bamboo trees, a voice clearly said, "Don't be afraid, Mande and Upik!"

Upik Manih and her mother, Mande, stood still and listened. The voice continued, "I do not want to scare you. I am not an evil human being who wants to disturb you. I was abandoned by my own parents. They were ashamed because I look like a snake."

The voice sounded very sad. Upik Manih and her mother felt pity. They decided not to run away and kept listening to the voice. "You should know that I have been here even when the bamboo tree was still a bamboo shoot. I am not able to move freely in this bamboo tree and I feel really tortured. I want to go out."

Upik Manih and her mother were still standing there not knowing what to do. The voice continued, "Every day I pray that somebody will cut me down and take me home. Apparently this bamboo tree is too big to be used for *lemang* mold. That is why both of you didn't choose this stem."

"Please help me Upik, please help me Mande. I can't bear it any more. Cut down this bamboo stem," the voice asked for compassion. But Upik Manih and her mother just kept standing there. They were confused. What should they do?

The voice said again, "Mande, Upik, please help me. Remove me immediately. Cut down this bamboo." The voice sounded very soft and was not scary any more.

Despite that, they still didn't dare to fulfill the request of the voice. Who knew whether a mean creature might be feigning kindness while actually intending to bring misfortune on them?

Finally the voice complained, "Perhaps this is my fate to always be buried here and never see the beautiful sun. I am always in darkness."

A few moments later Upik Manih mustered up the courage to ask, "Who are you? Are you a human being or a supernatural creature?"

"Upik Manih, I am an ordinary human being, but I have had an unfortunate fate. Since I was born, my skin has been scaly like a snake. Moreover, my body is thin and long. This is why my parents condemned and abandoned me in this big bamboo tree. Ever since then, I have been enslaved beneath the fourth joint of the bamboo," the voice explained.

Upik was still doubtful. Then the voice said again, "Please help me to be set free. I will repay your kindness. Believe me! It is only you who could release me."

Finally Upik Manih and her mother cut down the big bamboo tree and brought it home. They removed the snake and Upik made a case for the snake to live in. The snake was very grateful for the help he had received.

Every morning the snake sunbathed in the yard, and when the night came he would play under the moonlight and star rays. The snake was happy.

Day after day. Week after week. Month after month. Almost one year had the snake lived with Upik Manih and her mother. The snake had never troubled them. He was never capricious.

But since Upik Manih and her mother had begun to take care of the snake, the neighbors had started mocking them. One said that Upik Manih had married a snake, and another said that Upik Manih's brother was a snake. But they never paid attention to these rumors because they sincerely wanted to help the poor snake. They also never told anybody about the origin of the snake.

One night the snake dreamed of receiving a visit from his grandmother. The grandmother said, "My grandson, it is about time for you to be set free from the curse. Give your snake skin to Upik Manih. Ask her to burn it. There will be three explosions. Tell Upik Manih to ask anything she wants when the explosions sound. But tell her to ask for your release on the third explosion. Remember my message."

In the morning the poor snake told his dream to Upik Manih. He asked her to do what his grandmother had said in his dream. The kindhearted Upik Manih willingly fulfilled the snake's request. Immediately she burnt the snake's skin.

Three explosions sounded. On the first explosion, Upik Manih asked for a hill where bamboos would grow to make molds for *lemang*. (Purportedly this is the origin of Talang Mountain. *Talang* means bamboo in the local language.)

When the second explosion sounded, Upik Manih asked for a wide rice field. (According to the villagers, this is how the wide rice field came to exist at the foot of Talang Mountain in a regency called Solok.)

On the third explosion, Upik Manih pleaded for the release of the snake from his curse.

At first a thin fog covered the snake body. After the fog disappeared, a handsome and dashing youth was standing there.

The dashing youth was very grateful to the kindhearted Upik Manih. Now he was freed from his curse. As he had no name, Upik's mother called him Prince Bulueh.

Upik Manih then married Prince Bulueh. They lived happily and prosperously with the mother.

Note: *Lemang* is a traditional food of the Minangkabau people (in West Sumatera). Made from glutinous rice mixed with coconut milk, it is cooked in a length of bamboo that has been wrapped with banana leaves on the inside. The glutinous rice-filled bamboo shapes are lined up over a hearth. People usually make many of them at one time.

**Tame monkeys along the main street of Pusuk, near Senggigi Beach on
Lombok Island. Photograph by Murti Bunanta.**

MOTIFS AND TALE SOURCES

Prepared by Margaret Read MacDonald and Murti Bunanta

The following notes contain folklore motif numbers and descriptions. These motifs were created by folklorist Stith Thompson and are used by folklorists throughout the world to identify folktales. Thompson's motif index is published by the Indiana University Press as *Motif-Index of Folk-Literature* (1966). Two editions of a motif index of children's folktale collections are also cited: *The Storyteller's Sourcebook: A Subject, Title and Motif-Index to Children's Folklore Collections* by Margaret Read MacDonald (Gale Research, 1982) and *The Storyteller's Sourcebook: A Subject, Title and Motif Index to Children's Folklore Collections, 1983–1999* by Margaret Read MacDonald and Brian Sturm (Gale Research, 2001). Type numbers given are from Antti Aarne and Stith Thompson, *The Types of the Folktale: Folklore Fellows Communications, No. 184 (Suomalainen Tiedeakatenia, 1961).*

Tattadu (A Folktale from South Sulawesi). Collected in the Duri Massenrengpulu language. In this unusual tale the youngest of seven sisters says she will marry anyone, even a caterpillar: *B643.3 Marriage to person in caterpillar form.* A magic treasure pumpkin grows on the farm of Tattadu, the caterpillar: *D1463.2.1 Magic pumpkin furnishes treasure. D981.11 Magic pumpkin.* The caterpillar husband visits god and is forged into a handsome human: *D576 Transformation by being burned. D683.5 Transformation by god (goddess).* Tattadu is given a magic rice wine container that is never empty: *D1046 Magic wine; D1652.2 Inexhaustible drink.* Using this, he bets chiefs he meets that they cannot drain it, and he wins riches: *K264 Deceptive wager.* The jealous sisters send their husbands to be forged as well, but they are turned into animals: *J2415 Foolish imitation of lucky man.*

> **Source:** "Tattadu," in *Cerita Rakyat Daerah Sulawesi Selatan, Departemen Pendidikan dan Kebudayaan, Proyek Inventarisasi dan Dokumentasi Kebudayaan Daerah, Jakarta,* 1982. (*Folktales from South Sulawesi Province. Department of Education and Culture, Inventory and Documentation of Regional Culture Project, Jakarta,* 1982.)

Bujang Permai (A Folktale from Pasar Baru Regency in West Sumatra.) A delightful mixture of *Type 554 The Grateful Animals* and *Type 610 The Healing Fruits.* A young brother tells what he will do in future and is abandoned by his older brothers. This motif appears also in tales from India. *N234 Boast of poor boy made good by fate. He boasts to elder brothers he will build a palace on a certain spot: accidentally comes on treasure trove and makes good his boast.* A god appears to the boy in a dream and gives him seven magical palm leaf ribs, which revive the dead. *E64 Resuscitation by magic object.* He revives a squirrel, elephant, macaque, and firefly. *H346 Princess given to man who can heal her. B582.2 Animals help hero win princess. B360 Animals grateful for rescue from peril of death. H310 Suitor tests.* Elephant levels hill, squirrel and macaque pick and arrange betel leaves. Firefly identifies princess: *H162 Recognition of disguised princess by bee lighting on her. H1242 Youngest brother alone succeeds on quest. W11.13 Youngest brother shares wealth with older ones.* The motif of magic palm leaf ribs appears in two stories in this book but does not appear in Stith Thompson's index.

> *Source:* "Bujang Permai," in *Cerita Rakyat Daerah Sumatera Barat oleh Proyek Penelitian dan Pencatatan Kebudayaan Daerah, Departamen Pendidikan dan Kebudayaan, Proyek Penerbitan Buku Bacaan dan Sastra Indonesia dan Daerah, Jakarta, 1982. (Folktales from West Sumatera Province by Research and Registration of Regional Culture Project. Department of Education and Culture, Publication of Book on Indonesian and Regional Literature Project, Jakarta, 1978.)*

Molek (A Folktale from Riau Province). This is a lovely variant of *Type 413 Marriage by Stealing Clothing,* with female protagonist. Molek marries the fish, Jerawan: *B644 Marriage to person in fish form.* Takes his skin while he is in human form: *D721.2 Disenchantment by hiding skin (covering). D521 Transformation by putting on skin.* Learning his human name seems to help break the enchantment: *D511 Transformation by breaking name tabu.* Her sisters abandon her in a boat, but her husband rescues her: *K2212 Treacherous sisters.* Compare this tale with the Selkie tales of the British Isles (*MacDonald B651.8 Marriage to seal in human form; F302.4.2.2* Animal (bird) in maiden form comes into man's power when he hides her skin.*). See *MacDonald B644.1* Marriage to person in fish form, Muchie Lal,* for a variant of this tale from India. Find a Yoruba variant at *MacDonald B654 Marriage to fish in human form.*

> *Source:* "Si Molek dan Tanara," in *Cerita Rakyat Daerah Riau, Departemen Pendidikan dan Kebudayaan, Proyek Inventarisasi dan Dokumentasi Kebudayaan Daerah, Jakarta, 1982. (Folktales from Riau Province. Department of Education and Culture, Inventory and Documentation of Regional Culture Project, Jakarta, 1982.)*

The Three Brothers: A Folktale from Lampung Province. Youngest of three brothers says plans to sit on golden chair with diamond throne and beautiful carpet when grown. Elder brothers abandon him. He climbs tree and sees King of Wild Boars hang jewel necklace on tree: *B101.2 Treasure-hog. D1072 Magic necklace.* Wearing this magic necklace he finds he can walk on water: *D1841.4.3 Walking upon water without wetting the soles or garments.* Crosses to foreign country: *D1520.34 Transportation by means of necklace.* Is taken into palace to work. Is good worker and reliable person, so King marries daughter to him. Sits on golden chair with diamond throne and carpet: *N202 Wishes for good fortune realized. H1242 Youngest brother alone succeeds on quest.* Brothers arrive in kingdom, are recognized by Youngest and forgiven: *W11.14 Youngest brother shares with older ones.*

> *Source:* "*Anak Saudagar Telumuakhi Kera,*" in *Cerita Rakyat Daerah Lampung oleh Proyek Penelitian dan Pencatatan Kebudayaan Daerah, Departemen Pendidikan dan Kebudayaan, Proyek Penerbitan Buku Sastra Indonesia dan Daerah, Jakarta,* 1981. ("Children of Person of Rank," in *Folktales of Lampung Province by Research and Registration of Regional Culture Project. Department of Education and Culture, Project of Publication of Books on Indonesian and Regional Literature, Jakarta,* 1981.) Information on *dadih* was collected from Denny Djoenaid, a children's book illustrator and animator born in West Sumatera Province. His grandmother used to make *dadih.*

Princess White Hair (A Folktale from Perigi Village in South Sumatera Province). In this very unique motif the Princess spurns all suitors and turns their hair white by spitting on them: *D1001 Magic spittle. D1776 Magic results from spitting.* Her brother is assigned tasks, which his magic strength passes: *F610 Remarkably strong man. H1562 Test of strength. H1510 Tests of power to survive. Vain attempts to kill hero. H1535.1 Pit test.* Brother rescues princess and carries her off. Her hair bun falls, creating pool in river: *A934 Various origins of rivers.*

> *Source:* "Putri Rambut Putih," in *Cerita Rakyat Daerah Sumatera Selatan, Departemen Pendidikan dan Kebudayaan, Pusat Penelitian Sejarah dan Budaya, Proyek Penelitian dan Pencatatan Kebudayaan Daerah,* 1978/1979. (*Folktales from South Sumatera Province, Department of Education and Culture, Centre for History and Culture Research, Research and Registration Regional Culture Project,* 1978/1979.)

Princess Pinang Masak (A Folktale from Senuro Village in South Sumatera Province). This unusual motif appears also in the folklore of India. *K1821.7.1 Beautiful woman blackens face as disguise.* Princess Pinang Masak thus escapes marriage to the King, flees with her household, and wishes that girls of the village she founds should never be beautiful. *D1871 Girls magically made hideous.* Thus never put in her desperate position.

> *Source:* "Putri Pinang Masak," in *Cerita Rakyat Daerah Sumatera Selatan, Departemen Pendidikan dan Kebudayaan, Pusat Penelitian Sejarah dan Budaya, Proyek Penelitian dan Pencatatan Kebudayaan Daerah,* 1978/1979. (*Folktales from South Sumatera Province, Department of Education and Culture, Centre for History and Culture Research, Research and Registration Regional Culture Project,* 1978/1979.)

Princess Kemang (A Folktale from Bengkulu). Princess hunter (*F565 Women warriors or hunters*) follows deer into forest (*N773 Adventures from pursuing enchanted animal (hind, boar, bird)*, which turns into tiger (*D659.10 Transformation to lure hunters to certain place*). Tree to which she has been led turns into man enchanted as tree. *D431.2 Transformation: tree to person; D215.8 Transformation: man (woman) to mango tree.* En route home, princess encounters crocodiles and uses *Motif K579.2 Monkey in danger on bridge of crocodiles pretends that king has ordered them counted.* She counts crocs and crosses river. For more Indonesian variants of the croc crossing motif see MacDonald *K579.2.1** and MacDonald and Sturm *K579.2.1.*

> *Source:* "Putri Kemang," in *Cerita Rakyat Daerah Bengkulu. Departemen Pendidikan dan Kebudayaan, Proyek Inventarisasi dan Dokumentasi Kebudayaan Daerah, Jakarta, 1982. (Folktales from Bengkulu Province, Department of Education and Culture, Inventory and Documentation of Regional Culture Project, Jakarta, 1982.)*

The Legend of Malin Kundang (A Folktale from West Sumatera Province). Son Malin Kundang apprenticed to merchant. Becomes rich merchant. Refuses to recognize poor parents when sails back, though is recognized by scar on forehead: *H51 Recognition by scar. S21 Cruel son. P236 Undutiful children. W154 Ingratitude. W155 Hardness of heart.* Storm sinks his ship: *Q552.12 Punishment: shipwreck. Q552.13 Storm as punishment.* Wreckage turned to stones near Air Manis close to Padang: *A970 Origin of rocks and stones. A974 Rocks from transformation of people to stone: A977 Origin of particular stones or groups of stones.*

> *Source:* Murti Bunanta heard "Legenda Malin Kundang" for the first time from her mother when she was a child. Her late mother was born in Muntilan, Central Java, and shared many stories with her children, mostly Javanese folktales. Murti read several other variants during her childhood. But even though Malin Kundang is widely known among other cultures in Indonesia, Murti has only located it in twelve publications. This is fewer than other comparable folk stories. For discussion of this see Murti Bunanta, *Problematika Penulisan Cerita Rakyatuntuck anak di Indonesia* (Balai Pustaka, 1998), 7.

The Spoiled Little Kitten (A Folktale from Deli Serdang in North Sumatera Province). Siamese cat wants to be fed by mother. Seeks sun as mother, then mist, wind, hill, carabao, rattan, rat, and cat. This motif is popular in Asian folklore. See MacDonald and MacDonald and Sturm *Z42 Stronger and Strongest* and *L293 Mouse stronger than wall, wind, mountain* for many variants. The tale is often told of a stone-cutter, or of a mouse seeking a husband. This Indonesian variant is interesting for its use of a spoiled child as the protagonist. *S21 Cruel son.*

> *Source:* "Kucing Siam," in *Cerita Rakyat Daerah Sumatera Utara oleh Proyek Penelitian dan Pencatatan Kebudayaan Daerah, Departemen Pendidikan dan Kebudayaan, Proyek Penerbitan Buku Bacaan dan Sastra Indonesia dan*

Daerah, Jakarta, 1978. ("Siamese Cat," in *Folktales from North Sumatera Province by Research and Registration of Regional Culture Project, Department of Education and Culture, Project of Publication of Books on Indonesian and Regional Literature, Jakarta,* 1978.)

Sikintan (A Folktale from Jamu Region in Aceh Province). Father dreams of diamond stick, finds it in bamboo cluster. *N531 Treasure discovered through dream.* Sends son to other island to sell stick, becomes merchant and becomes rich. Dreams of parents: *J156.2 Fate of parents revealed in dream.* Returns home but is embarrassed to recognize parents: *S21 Cruel son. Q281.1 Ungrateful children punished. W155 Hardness of heart.* Typhoon punishes his ship: *Q552.13 Storm as punishment.* Turns back. Still cannot bear to accept raggedy parents. Typhoon destroys ship. Parents curse to have no blessing from them or from heavens: *M411.1 Curse by parent. Q442.12 Punishment: shipwreck.* Island with white monkey appears, known as Si Kintan's island now: *A1715.5 Animals from transformed survivors of shipwreck. A1617 Origin of place-name.*

Source: "Sikintan," in *Cerita Rakyat Daerah Istimewa Aceh oleh Proyek Penelitian dan Pencatatan Kebudayaan Daerah, Departemen Pendidikan dan Kebudayaan, Proyek Penerbitan Buku Sastra Indonesia dan Daerah, Jakarta,* 1981. ("Sikintan," in *Folktales from Aceh Province by Research and Registration of Regional Culture Project, Department of Education and Culture, Project of Publication of Books on Indonesian and Regional Culture, Jakarta,* 1981.)

Rawa Tekuluk (A Folktale from West Sumatera). Spoiled girl will not help mother carry rice home from field. Sent back for it, she buries it in mud, says could not find: *W111.5.2 Lazy girl does not know where the spring is.* Mother discovers and curses girl, leaving her in swamp: *M411.1 Curse by parent.* She sinks: *Q321 Laziness punished.* Q281.1 Ungrateful children punished. Shawl left, hence name of swamp (shawl swamp): *A1617 Origin of place-name.*

Source: "Rawa Tekuluk," in *Cerita Rakyat Daerah Sumatera Barat oleh Proyek Penelitian dan Pencatatan Kebudayaan Daerah, Departemen Pendidikan dan Kebudayaan, Proyek Penerbitan Buku Bacaan dan Sastra Indonesia dan Daerah, Jakarta, 1978.* ("Swamp of the Shawl," in *Folktales from West Sumatera Province by Research and Registration of Regional Culture, Department of Education and Culture, Project of Publication of Books on Indonesian and Regional Literature, Jakarta,* 1978.)

Batu Badaung: The Story of Ungrateful Children (A Folktale from Ulath Village on Saparua Island in Central Maluku). Ungrateful children eat up all of small amount of food and leave nothing for mother: *S20.2 Child hides food from starving parents. S20 Cruel children and grandchildren.* She sings to stone to swallow her: *D1552 Mountains or rocks open and close. F800 Extraordinary rocks and stones. D931 Magic rock (stone):* Little girl calls for stone to spit out mother. She is carried to shore by wave. Stone never emerges from sea again: *A970 Origin of certain stone. D2153.1 Rock in sea created by magic. Q281.1 Ungrateful children punished.*

Source: This story was collected from Frans Hitipeuw, born in 1938 in Saparua, Central Maluku. He heard this story from his ancestors. He wrote many publications on Moluccas culture and customs and had a degree in education from the University of Indonesia. According to Frans, a song based on this story was recorded on a gramophone in 1948, created by Kace Hehanusa with his band Rindu Alam. This story is also one of the most well known among people in other parts of Indonesia.

Why Rice Grains Are So Small (A Folktale from West Kalimantan). A motif popular in European folklore appears within this story: the cooking pot that will not cease overflowing. *C916.3 Magic porridge-pot keeps cooking. . . . It fills house with porridge and will not stop.* In this case it is a forgetful daughter who cannot remember the correct amount of rice to add to the pot. Compare with the Italian tale, *Stregga Nonna* by Tomie de Paola. *D973.1 Magic rice-grains. A1423.2 Acquisition of rice.*

Source: This story was collected from Getruda Trusaka when she was twenty-six years old. She heard this story as a child from her grandfather, Stephanus Adjong, now eighty years old a child. Stephanus was born in Entuma village, Sanggar Kapuas, in Kalimantan. Trusaka is a secretary for Yayasan Perhimpunan Rindang Banua, a foundation that works for all ethnic groups in Kalimantan.

The Origin of Rice in Java Island (A Folktale from Central Java). An unusual tale in which a youth goes to heaven to learn how to grow rice, then steals grains. Dewi Sri, Goddess of Rice, allows him to keep it if humans follow all her prescriptions about the crop. *K311 Thief in disguise. A433.1.1 God of rice fields. A1423.2 Acquisition of rice.* Humans never allowed in heaven again. *C955 Banishment from heaven for breaking tabu.*

Source: This story was collected from G. M. Sudarta, a children's book illustrator and political cartoonist. He heard this story from the farmers who lived near his home when he was a child growing up in Klaten. Nowadays the story is sometimes still performed in remote villages.

The Origin of Rice (A Folktale from Flores, West Nusa Tenggara Province). *D214.1 Transformation: man (woman) to rice-grains. A2685 Origin of cereals. A2685.6* (MacDonald). Origin of rice.* An unusual version of the human-to-rice plant tradition, in this tale a sister asks her brothers to kill her, mince her body, and scatter her all over the field. Rice grows as a result.

Source: This story was collected from Simon Sibon Ola, a lecturer in the Faculty of Education and Arts at the University of Nusa Cendana in East Nusa Tenggara. He heard this story from a farmer, Sina Kelen, who lives in Sinamalaka village, East Flores. In the past this story was told only as part of the ceremony before planting rice.

The Origin of Rice (A Folktale from Central Kalimantan Province). Princess gives self as sacrifice to bring rains; rice plants grow from field where her blood flowed. *S263.3 Person sacrificed to water spirit to secure water supply. D214.1 Transformation: man (woman) to rice-grain. D965.8.1 Magic rice (plant). D2157.2.0.1 Rice grows in single day. A2685.6* (MacDonald)* Origin of rice.

> *Source:* "Asal Mula Padi," in *Cerita Rakyat Daerah Kalimantan Tengah, Departemen Pendidikan dan Kebudayaan, Proyek Inventarisasi dan Dokumentasi Kebudayaan Daerah, Jakarta , 1982.* ("The Origin of Rice," in *Folktales from Central Kalimantan Province, Department of Education and Culture, Inventory and Documentation of Regional Culture Project, Jakarta, 1982.*)

How Rice Grows in the Wet Rice Field (A Folktale from Central Sulawesi Province). This unusual tale bears similarity to *N831.1 Mysterious housekeeper.* In that motif a man usually finds his housework magically done, catches the worker, and weds her. In this case it is a magical hero (*N838 Hero (culture hero) as helper*) who causes the girl's rice to grow. They wed and she takes in the six older sisters who had rejected her. *P252.3 Seven sisters.*

> *Source:* "Asal Mula Padi," in *Kumpulan Cerita tentang Padi. Balai Kajian Sejarah dan Nilai-Nilai Tradisional, jogyakarta, 1961.* ("The Origin of Rice," in *Collection of Stories on Rice, Centre for Study of History and Traditional Value, Jogyakarta, 1961.*)

The Origin of the Name of Kundi Village (A Folktale from Bangka-Belitung Province). Village named for dropped hair pin of visiting Javanese women. *A1617 Origin of place-name.*

> *Source:* This story was collected by Murti Bunanta in 2002 from Judhy Syarofie, a thirty-one-year-old journalist, who heard this story on a recent visit to Kundi village from a villager who had heard it from his ancestors.

Why Goat Eats Grass (A Folktale from East Nusa Tenggara). Told in the Dawan language. Unkind monkey (*K2297 Treacherous friend*) refuses to share fruit with goat below. Goat eats grass thereafter. *A2435.3 Food of various animals—mammals.*

> *Source:* Murti got this story in 2001 from Occa da Lima Meak, then aged twenty-six, who works in a public hospital in Kefamenanu, a small town in East Nusa Tenggara. She used to hear this story when she was between three and ten years old from her grandfather, Bae Usi, who was seventy years old in 2001. He usually told stories to his grandchildren during the full moon or when he put them to bed.

Why Shrimps Are Crooked (A Folktale from Central Kalimantan Province). Fish take turns cooking. Each jumps in pot and lays eggs, then boils for lunch. Shrimp tries to imitate, misunderstands, and boils *self* in pot. *J2401 Fatal imitation. J2415.3 Crab tries to imitate bird who lays eggs in pot of boiling water. Falls in instead of being rewarded.* Why shrimp is red and has crooked back. *A2411.5.7 Color of shrimp. A2356.2.15* (MacDonald) Why shrimp has broken back.*

> *Source:* "Udang Yang Bodoh," in *Cerita Rakyat Daerah Kalimantan Tengah, Proyek Penelitian dan Pencatatan Kebudayaan Daerah, Pusat Penelitian Sejarah dan Budaya Departemen Pendidikan dan Kebudayaan,* 1978/1979. ("The Stupid Shrimp," in *Folktales from Central Kalimantan Province, Research and Registration of Regional Culture Project, Center of Research on History and Culture, Department of Education and Culture,* 1978/1979.)

The Origin of the Banyan Tree. In some places the banyan tree has been considered sacred, especially in the islands that experienced Hindu influences, including Java, Madura, and Bali. The tree is looked upon as the abode of both good and bad spirits. In the Stith Thompson motif index, the story is *A2681.10. Origin of Banyan Tree.*

> *Source:* "De legende van den Waringin Boom, Javaansche Sagen, Mythen en Legenden"—*versameld door* [collected by] Jos Meyboom—Italiaander, Tweede herziene Druk [second edition], Zutphen—W.J. Thieme & Cie [publisher], MCMXXVIII [1928] and Murti Bunanta, *Legenda Pohon Beringin* (*The Legend of the Banyan Tree*) (Jakarta: Kelompok Pencinta Bacaan Anak, 2001).

The Origin of the Trunyan People (A Folktale from Bali Province). This unusual tale includes the motif of a magically fragrant tree that draws the gods to it: *D1599.2 Air magically made fragrant. D950 Magic tree:* One of the gods marries the goddess who guards the tree: *A164 Marriage or liaison of gods.* And the place name results from the tree's name "taru menyan." *A1617 Origin of place-name.*

> *Source:* This story was collected from Made Taro, a Balinese folktale writer, graduate in archeology, and founder of a children's theater, *Sanggar Kukuruyuk,* in 1979, in which he creates children's plays and songs based on folktales. He heard this story in 1967 from Nengah Tekes, a villager in Trunyan who inherited the story from his ancestors. A statue named Datonta is found in Trunyan. It is assumed that it was built in the tenth century and is believed to be the depiction of the god in the story.

The Legend of Toba Lake (A Folktale from North Sumatera Province). This tale casts a magical fish in the role of *N831.1 Mysterious Housekeeper.* The motif of a young man who brings home a magical animal that changes form while he is gone and keeps house for him is found throughout the world. Usually the magical wife vanishes when the husband violates her tabu by revealing her secret, or when her secret attribute (wings, skin) is discovered. This tale ends with a motif that is found in several Indonesian tales, the breaking forth of a spring. *F933.6 Spring miraculously bursts forth against wrong-doer. A920.1.8.1 Lake from violating tabu. A930 Origin of stream.*

> *Source:* Murti read several books and comics relating this story when she was a child. The story presented here is her retelling and interpretation from those materials.

The Legend of a Hill: Bukit Kelam (A Folktale from West Kalimantan Province).
A962.10 Hill represents loads from culture-hero's shoulders. A963 Mountains from stones (soil, sand) dropped or thrown.

> *Source:* This story was collected in 2001 from Aloysius Aloy, a former member of the House of Representatives, then fifty-nine years old. He heard this story for the first time when he was a child. He heard a more detailed version on his visit to the people of Sintang in 1998. Aloysius is a prominent Dayak Sanggau figure.

The Legend of a Swamp: Rawa Bening (A Folktale from Central Java).
This tale includes an unusual variant of *D191 Transformation: man to serpent (snake).* A hermit's son with ugly face changes into a snake, is cut unwittingly by villagers, turns into scar-faced boy and is rebuffed by villagers. *Q295.2 Cruelty to sick persons punished. Q286 Uncharitableness punished. F933.6 Spring miraculously bursts forth against wrongdoer. A920.1.8.1 Lake from violating tabu.*

> *Source:* Murti heard this story many times from her mother and liked to visit the swamp with her father when she was a child. In the story as given here, Murti has added some details from other sources. This legend is very popular among the Javanese people.

The Legend of a Stone: Batu Pelanduk (A Folktale from East Kalimantan Province).
This tale combines two distinct folk characters, the giant, Bengkaal, and the trickster mouse deer, Kancil. Bengkaal is moving stones about in the river. *A977.1 Giant responsible for certain stones.* Kancil stops him by a false threat. *K1700 Deception through bluffing. K1710 Ogre (large animal) overawed.*

> *Source:* Murti got this story in 2001 from Flora A. Moerdani, then sixty-two years old. Flora works for the promotion of East Kalimantan culture and arts. She heard this story through an interview with a traditional medicine expert, a man named Ting Juan, on her visit to the spot where the stones lie. All the people of Dayak Bakau know about this story.

The Legend of a City: Banyuwangi (A Folktale from East Java Province). This tale contains motifs *S322 Children abandoned (driven forth, exposed) by hostile relative. S322.6 Jealous mother-in-law and sisters cast woman's children forth. K2116.1.1 Innocent woman accused of killing her new-born children* and *N271.6 Murder revealed by child.* Also *F932 Extraordinary occurrences connected with rivers.* Stith Thompson shows no tracings for the unusual motif of a sweet-smelling river.

> *Source:* This is another story Murti heard from her mother when she was a child.

The Legend of Sembra River (A Folktale from East Irian Jaya Province in the Tehit Language). Stith Thompson does not cite the specific tabu on using *renat* leaves to wrap food. *C219 Tabu: eating from certain place.* The breaking of this tabu is punished by *F933.6 Spring miraculously breaks forth against wrongdoers. A934.7 River bursts from well in pursuit. A930 Origin of stream.* And *A974 Rocks from transformation of people to stones.* It is interesting to see this motif of punishment by a flood used in Irian Jaya as well as in many Indonesian islands. The tale includes a tag ending *A2681 Origin of trees,* caused by Serefle's calls for help. The tale carries a moral that one should not bear resentments against friends. *C881 Tabu: grumbling.*

> *Source:* "Serefle," in *Cerita Rakyat Daerah Irian Jaya, Departemen Pendidikan dan Kebudayaan, Proyek Inventarisasi dan Dokumentasi Kebudayaan Daerah, Jakarta, 1983.* ("Serefle," in *Folktales from Irian Jaya Province (now Papua), Department of Education and Culture, Inventory and Documentation of Regional Culture Project, Jakarta,* 1983.)

The Origin of a Mountain: Talang Mountain (A Folktale from West Sumatera Region). *D191 Transformation: man to serpent (snake).* The snake is returned to human form through a combination of burning the skin (*D721.3 Disenchantment by destroying skin (covering)*) and wishing the snake back into human form (*D521 Transformation through wish*). *Type 433 The Prince as Serpent.*

> *Source:* This story was collected in 2001 from Ronidin, then twenty-five years old, a student in the Faculty of Letters at Andalas University, Padang, West Sumatera. He heard this story for the first time from his late grandmother, Suli, at bedtime. Often afterwards his grandmother told this story in gatherings with his friends after sunset prayers. Information on *lemang* is given by Yusrizal KW, a short story writer, activist in promoting the culture of West Sumatera, and the chairperson of Citra Budaya Indonesia Foundation, which works for the preservation of the culture.

GLOSSARY

Abug: cake

Adat: local custom

Agar Agar: white seaweed product used in making pudding

Agar Agar Santan: coconut milk pudding

Alih-alihan: hide and seek game from Bali

Andep: help, assistance

Ani-ani: small palm-held knife for reaping rice

Awo: rattan plant

Badaung: leafy; something that has leaves

Bae kean: friendship call in the Dawan language

Bahasa: language

Bala-Bala Tumban: children's game

Balanga: earthen cooking pot

Balida: very bony fish about as big as the palm of the hand

Banta: white fish with black spots, as big as the palm of the hand

Banyan: large tree with hanging tendrils that take root when they reach the ground, creating a virtual forest from one tree

Banyu: water

Barong: costumed dance from Bali

Batik: fabric decorated by waxing certain areas and dipping in dyes, repeating until pattern is created, or by drawing or printing on fabric.

Batik cap: printed batik

Batik tulis: batik created by drawing with special tool

Batu: stone

Belo: monkey

Bening: clear

Beringin: banyan tree

Bhinneka: diversity

Bibi: goat

Biji: seed

Bintang: star

Bintang Waluku: Orion

Bukit: hill

Carabao: water buffalo

Datu: title of headman

Dayak: largest ethnic group living in Kalimantan

Dewi: goddess

Dewi Sri: goddess of wet rice

Didong: storytelling style of Gayo people in Aceh, North Sumatera

Gabus: similar to a catfish; scaly with black dots

Gado-gado: cooked mixed vegetables with peanut sauce

Gamelan: music played on sets of metal instruments: some small gongs, some metal xylophone-style instruments

Gantang: measure of rice equivalent to 6.875 lbs (3.125kg)

Garu: harrow for rice fields

Granat: grenade

Hoho: storytelling style of Ono Niha in Nias Island

Ika: one

Ikat: elaborate woven cloth

Iris: slice or a very thin slice

Jackfruit: huge fruit that hangs from the trunk of a large tree, with soft yellow pulp surrounding large seeds, and knobbly skin.

Kaba: storytelling style of Minangkabau in West Sumatra

Kecil: small

Kendali: dirt

Kenduri: ritual meal

Keong gondang: large snail

Keris: dagger imbued with magical strength

Ketoprak: (1) Javanese dance drama; (2) Jakarta area salad consisting of bean sprouts, tofu, rice noodles, and peanut sauce

Ketupat: steamed rice wrapped in woven coconut leaves

Koba-koba: important tool for Tehit people; can be used as a bag, umbrella, or mat

Konde: pin for hair bun

Kring-Kringan: hide and seek game of Northern Bali

Kue: cake

Kue Biji Nangka: cake that takes the form of jackfruit seed

Kundang: spoiled

Lele: catfish

Lemang: rice cake molded in a length of bamboo

Lesung: rice mortar

Lontar: palmyra palm, the leaves of which can be written on

Macan: tiger

Mahabarata: classical Indian epic

Mandep: tradition of shared work (n.); to help (v.)

Meduni: ceremony before planting rice

Meru: pagoda

Muncrat: spurt

Nangka: See Jackfruit

Nasi goreng: fried rice with delicious tidbits stirred in

Obak Dele: hide and seek game of East Java

Orang: human

Padi: rice

Pallawa: South Indian script

Pancasila: creed adopted by Indonesian government; guarantees freedom of religion.

Patin: gray fish about 9.85 inches (25 cm) long, with soft bones and rich meat

Pelanduk: mouse deer

Periuk: cooking pot

Petak Umpet: hide and seek game of Lampung

Pomelo: kind of grapefruit

Ramayana: classical Indian epic of Rama and Sita

Rattan: type of tropical plant with a strong stem that is easily bent

Rawa: swamp

Renat: creeping plant, It is tabu to use the leaf of the renat plant to wrap woodworms, sago, or pork.

Rentak: sinking

Saluang: small white fish about 1.97 inches (5 cm) long

Sam Khong: hide and seek game of West Kalimantan

Satai: small pieces of meat barbecued on a stick

Satay: small pieces of meat barbecued on a stick

Satu: one

Sawah: wet rice fields

Sekampil: measurement made by touching the thumb to the index finger

Sengge: children's game

Sepat: gray fish about the length of a hand, used dried

Sewuli: measurement made by touching the thumbs and index fingers of both hands together

Sodo: palm leaf rib

Songket: textile with gold or silver threads

Sukat: measurement; one sukat is 27.5 pounds (12.5 kilograms)

Talang: bamboo in West Sumatran language

Tamulilingan: bees with black bodies and yellow wings

Taru menyan: particularly fragrant tree

Tattadu: caterpillar

Tekuluk: shawl

Telan: eel-like fish with no scales; can reach length of an arm

Tomat: tomatoe

Tong Mok: hide and seek game of Ambarawa, Central Java

Tunggal: one and only

Ubi: sweet potato

Ucing Sumput: hide and seek game of West Java

Ulap Doyo: textile made from leaf fiber of the Doyo plant.

Ulos: textile made from pineapple fiber

Waluku: wooden plow used to turn over the soil in rice fields

Wangi: fragrant

Wayang golek: carved wooden rod puppets

Wayang klitik: doll puppet theater

Wayang kulit: flat, leather shadow puppets

Wayang orang: dance drama using humans to act out wayang puppet stories

Wayang sasak: flat leather shadow puppets used to perform Islamic stories

Wayang topeng: mask drama

Wedang tomat: hot tomato drink

Wellah: oar

Wiwit: rice harvest ceremony

BIBLIOGRAPHY

Aarne, Antti, and Stith Thompson. *The Types of the Folktale.* Helsinki: Suomalainen Tiedeakatemia, 1973.

Bellwood, Peter. "Austronesian Languages and Population Movements." In *Ancient History,* vol. 1 of *Indonesian Heritage.* Jakarta: Buku Antar Bangsa, 1996.

———. "Ceremonial Bronzes of the Pre-Classic Era." In *Ancient History,* vol. 1. of *Indonesian Heritage.* Jakarta: Buku Antar Bangsa, 1996.

Bengkulu Regional Office of Public Works. *Bengkulu Tourism Map, Sumatera—Indonesia.* Bengkulu: Local Government of Bengkulu, n.d.

Buku Masakan Indonesia—Mustika Rasa. *Buku Masakan Indonesia—Mustika Rasa.* Jakarta: Departemen Pertanian, 1967.

Bunanta, Murti. *Problematika Penulisan Cerita Rakyatunuk anak di Indonesia.* Jakarta: Balai Pustaka, 1998.

Danandjaja, James. "Indonesian Storytellers and Storytelling." In *Traditional Storytelling Today: An International Sourcebook*, edited by Margaret Read MacDonald. Chicago: Fitzroy Dearborn, 1999.

Discovery Channel. *Insight Guide—Indonesia.* Singapore: Apa Publications, 2001.

Kelompok Kerja Visi Anak Bangsa. *Report Paper on Warwut Village in South East Maluku Province.* Jakarta: Visi Anak Bangsa, 2000.

———. *Research Report on Ambarawa Village in Central Java.* Jakarta: Visi Anak Bangsa, 2000.

———. *Research Report on Bunaken Village in North Sulawesi Province.* Jakarta: Visi Anak Bangsa, 2000.

———. *Research Report on Kotogadang Village in West Sumatera Province.* Jakarta: Visi Anak Bangsa, 2000.

———. *Research Report on La'bo Village in South Sulawesi Province.* Jakarta: Visi Anak Bangsa, 2000.

———. *Research Report on Lamalera Village in East Nusa Tenggara Province.* Jakarta: Visi Anak Bangsa, 2000.

————. *Research Report on Pematangkabau Village in Jambi Province.* Jakarta: Visi Anak Bangsa, 2000.

————. *Research Report on Penyengat Village in Riau Province.* Jakarta: Visi Anak Bangsa, 2000.

————. *Research Report on Pesantren Tebuireng in East Java.* Jakarta: Visi Anak Bangsa, 2000.

————. *Research Report on Sepuluh Ilir Village in Palembang.* Jakarta: Visi Anak Bangsa, 2000.

————. *Research Report on Tanjung Isuy Village in East Kalimantan.* Jakarta: Visi Anak Bangsa, 2000.

Kong, Lily. "Bali." In *The Human Environment,* vol. 2 of *Indonesian Heritage.* Jakarta: Buku Antara Bangsa, 1996.

————. "Java." In *The Human Environment,* vol. 2 of *Indonesian Heritage.* Jakarta: Buku Antar Bangsa, 1996.

MacDonald, Margaret Read. *The Storyteller's Sourcebook: A Subject, Title, and Motif-Index to Folklore Collections for Children.* Detroit: Gale Research, 1982.

MacDonald, Margaret Read, and Brian W. Sturm. *The Storyteller's Sourcebook: A Subject, Title, and Motif-Index to Folklore Collections for Children, 1983–1999.* Detroit: Gale Research, 2001.

Melalatoa, Junus. *Saudara Sebangsa Setanah Air di Pulau-Pulau Kecil* (*Brothers in One Nation and Country in Small Islands*). Jakarta: Balai Pustaka, 1996.

Miksic, John. "The Kingdom of Majapahit." In *Ancient History,* vol. 1 of *Indonesian Heritage.* Jakarta: Buku Antar Bangsa, 1996.

Profil Propinsi Republik Indonesia. *Profile of the Provinces of Indonesian Republic.* Jakarta: Yayasan Bhakti Wawasan Nusantara, 1992.

Rigg, Jonathan. "Making Sense of Indonesia." In *The Human Environment,* vol. 2 of *Indonesian Heritage.* Jakarta: Buku Antar Bangsa, 1996.

Riwut, Cilik. *Kalimantan Membangun—Alam dan Kebudayaan* (*Building Kalimantan—Nature and Culture*). Jogyakarta: PT. Tiara Wacana Jogya, 1993.

Sedyawati, Edi. "Adoption of Buddhism and Hinduism." In *Ancient History,* vol. 1 of *Indonesian Heritage.* Jakarta: Buku Antar Bangsa, 1996.

————. "The Kingdoms of Kadiri and Singasari." In *Ancient History,* vol. 1 of *Indonesian Heritage.* Jakarta: Buku Antar Bangsa, 1996.

Soekmono, R. *Sedjarah Kebudayaan Indonesia* (*The History of Indonesian Culture*), vol. 1. Jakarta: Penerbit Nasional Trikarya, 1958.

Soemadio, Bambang. "Phases of Early Indonesian History." In *Ancient History,* vol. 1 of *Indonesian Heritage.* Jakarta: Buku Antar Bangsa, 1996.

Suprapti et al. *Persepsi Anak Didik Terhadap Lingkungan Tempat Tinggal di Klaten* (*Children's Perception Towards Their Living Environment in Klaten*). Jakarta: Departemen Pendidikan dan Kebudayaan (Department of Education and Culture), 1992.

Taro, Made. "Datonta—Dewa Tertinggi Masyarakat Trunyan" ("Datonta—The Highest God of Trunyan Society"). *Suluh Marhaen Magazine* 324 (1970): 2.

Thompson, Stith. *Motif-Index of Folk-Literature*. Bloomington: Indiana University Press, 1966.

Yasaboga, *Kue-Kue Indonesia* (*Indonesian Cakes*). Jakarta: PT. Gramedia Pustaka Utama, 1997.

Yusnono, P. "Peranan Strategis Yang Semestinya Diperankan Dewan Adat" ("The Appropriate Strategic Role of the Custom Boards"). In *Kebudayaan Dayak—Aktualisasi danTransformasi* (*Dayak Culture—Actualization and Transformation*), edited by Paulus Florus et al. Jakarta: Grasindo, 1994.

Picture Books

Bunanta, Murti. *The Legend of the Banyan Tree—Folktale from Central Java Province*. Jakarta: Kelompok Pencinta Bacaan Anak, 2001.

———. *The Mouse Deer and The Turtle—Folktale from West Kalimantan Province*. Jakarta: Kelompok Pencinta Bacaan Anak, 2001.

———. *Princess Jasmine—Folktale from North Sumatera Province*. Jakarta: Kelompok Pencinta Bacaan Anak, 2001.

———. *Senggutru—Folktale from Central Java Province*. Jakarta: Kelompok Pencinta Bacaan Anak, 2001.

———. *Si Molek—Folktale from Riau Province*. Jakarta: Kelompok Pencinta Bacaan Anak, 2001.

———. *Suwidak Loro—Folktale from Central Java*. Jakarta: Kelompok Pencinta Bacaan Anak, 2001.

———. *Tiny Boy—Folktale from South Sulawesi Province*. Jakarta: Kelompok Pencinta Bacaan Anak, 2001.

———. *The Youngest Frog—Folktale from Kei Island, Maluku*. Jakarta: Balai Pustaka, 1997.

Harjana, HP. *Topitu, the Angel from Heaven—Folktale from Central Sulawesi Province*. Jakarta: Kelompok Pencinta Bacaan Anak, 2001.

Sukanta, Putu Oka. *The Yellow Eggplant—Folktale from Bali*. Jakarta: Kelompok Pencinta Bacaan Anak, 2001.

Suyadi. *The Eclipse—Folktale from East Java Province*. Jakarta: Kelompok Pencinta Bacaan Anak, 2001.

————. *Joko Kendil, The Rice Pot—Folktale from Java.* Jakarta: Kelompok Pencinta Bacaan Anak, 2001.

————. *Made and His Four Best Friends—Folktale from Bali.* Jakarta: Kelompok Pencinta Bacaan Anak, 2001.

————. *The Mouse Deer and The King of Jungle—Folktale from Java.* Jakarta: Kelompok Pencinta Bacaan Anak, 2001.

————. *Timun Mas—Folktale from Java.* Jakarta: Balai Pustaka, 1997.

Taro, Made. *Onion and Garlic—Folktale from Bali.* Jakarta: Balai Pustaka, 1997.

INDEX

ABOUT THE AUTHOR, EDITOR, AND ILLUSTRATOR

Murti Bunanta is the first person to receive a doctorate from the University of Indonesia using research in children's literature as the topic for her dissertation. She is also the founder and President of *Kelompok Pencinta Bacaan Anak,* The Society for the Advancement of Children's Literature, (1987), a non-profit organization that pioneers various activities to develop children's reading in Indonesia. She has written a number of essays and given numerous lectures on children's literature abroad and at home. She has also written ten picture books based on folktales. Her first book entitled *Si Bungsu Katak* (1997) received The Janusz Korczak International Literary Prize Honorary Award, 1998 in Poland. Murti teaches storytelling and children's literature at the University of Indonesia–Jakarta. Murti single handedly has arranged for

Photograph by Endang Roh Suciati.

production of 15 beautifully illustrated folktale picture books from many provinces in Indonesia, pairing authors and illustrators. Her aim is to provide the children of Indonesia with a beautifully illustrated folktale from each of their provinces. One of these books, *The Legend of the Banyan Tree (2001)* received the award *Octagones 2002* for *Reflets d'Imaginaire d'Ailleurs* in France.

Dr. Margaret Read MacDonald met Murti Bunanta during two Indonesian storytelling tours organized by Dr. Bunanta. MacDonald, who holds a Ph.D. in Folklore from Indiana University, is the author of over thirty books on folklore and storytelling topics. She tours widely offering her "Playing with Story" performances and workshops and was a recent Fulbright Scholar in Thailand. In editing this collection, MacDonald has tried to keep the texts in Murti Bunanta's voice.

G. M. Sudarta has been a cartoonist for *Kompas Daily–Jakarta* since 1967 and served on the international jury for children's book illustration for the Hans Christian Andersen Award of IBBY in 1994. He has also taken part in international exhibitions and been a speaker for cartoon seminars both in Indonesia and abroad. G. M. Sudarta has illustrated several picture books.